The Curse of Pharaoh

"As Dickinson famously penned, 'tell the truth, but tell it slant.' Suehr does just that, artfully accompanying readers through those pesky eternal quandaries surrounding the nature of good and evil and what it means to be a human in this messy world of ours. *The Curse of Pharoah* is a wonderful offering for both individual and small group reflection, using humorous, down-to-earth illustrations to contemplate the hard questions. So 'let my people go' read this book!"

—ANNABELLE PEAKE MARKEY, Founder, Journeying Together, LLC

"In *The Curse of Pharaoh*, Chris Suehr moves from a toddler's persistent 'Why?' through the foibles of the Pharoah of Exodus to a destination of insight destined to become the origin of still more ventures. With wit and whimsy and a serious intellect unwilling to take itself too seriously, he has crafted a unique work that is simultaneously journey and map, reminding the reader that life is not certain and happiness is not inevitable, but that a rich experience of both is always available to the sincere seeker—or the self-aware Pharaoh."

—BRIAN MAAS, Vice President for Mission and Spiritual Care, Immanuel Senior Living

"Who are we who suffer? With his *The Curse of Pharaoh*, Chris Suehr invites the reader along a delightfully refreshing and accessible path of reflection. Through thoughtful exploration of the biblical character of Pharaoh, Suehr meditates anew upon life's perennial questions: Who are we? Why do we suffer? And how do we construct meaning out of that suffering? His insights provoke a reassessment of our casual assumptions concerning individuality and its relations to community and cosmos."

—VERNON W. CISNEY, Associate Professor of Interdisciplinary Studies, Gettysburg College

"Suehr's approach to this conversation about the realities of suffering, character, and villainy is presented in a simple, and yet profound, way. The conversation questions for each chapter make this an easily accessible text for book clubs and adult forums in faith groups. An outstanding opportunity to examine one's position within the deeper meaning of this Old Testament text's story of Pharoah—and in many ways most of us are a part of Suehr's description of the follies of Pharoah!"

    —DEACON NANCY E GABLE, Director of Admissions and Adjunct Faculty, United Lutheran Seminary

The Curse of Pharaoh

Suffering, Character, and Villainy

CHRIS SUEHR

WIPF & STOCK · Eugene, Oregon

THE CURSE OF PHARAOH
Suffering, Character, and Villainy

Copyright © 2025 Chris Suehr. All rights reserved. Except for brief quotations in critical publications or reviews, no part of this book may be reproduced in any manner without prior written permission from the publisher. Write: Permissions, Wipf and Stock Publishers, 199 W. 8th Ave., Suite 3, Eugene, OR 97401.

Wipf & Stock
An Imprint of Wipf and Stock Publishers
199 W. 8th Ave., Suite 3
Eugene, OR 97401

www.wipfandstock.com

PAPERBACK ISBN: 979-8-3852-4806-3
HARDCOVER ISBN: 979-8-3852-4807-0
EBOOK ISBN: 979-8-3852-4808-7

Dedication
Thanks, Mom and Dad.

So many songs unsung; so many books unwritten.
– The final words I heard from SKH

Table of Contents

Preface: In Retrospect xi

Prologue: The Bus Station 1

PART I: SUFFERING QUESTIONS

Chapter 1: What Things 7
Chapter 2: The Ways of Whence 18
Chapter 3: The Steps of How 27
Chapter 4: The Cliffs of Why 38
Chapter 5: The Summit of Who 44

PART II: CHARACTER AND VILLAINY

Chapter 6: If Only 57
Chapter 7: Pharaoh Pharaoh 63
Chapter 8: The Mighty 71
Chapter 9: Diligent Blips 83
Chapter 10: Crash and Foam 92
Chapter 11: Life in the Wake 101

Epilogue: Birth and Rebirth 107
Conversation Questions 111

Preface: In Retrospect

THIS BOOK IS THE dream of a younger me. Over a decade ago, I had my first book-sized thought. It took shape as much of my writing does, through jots on Post-its, napkins, and pamphlets. My best friend and I often joke: *Scraps turn into papers; papers turn into books. You buy 'em. You read 'em. Period.*

I owe great thanks to those who have chatted about the ideas in here (Angela most of all but many more), who read this manuscript (Annabelle, Jeanne, Clif), and who have supported me in the process (Ramona, Maya, and Janet). They all helped these scraps of ideas become better words.

It seems like everyone I know has hopes to write a book, but life gets in the way. Ideas feel so big in your head but look so small in print.

A younger guy wrote most of this book. He was full of hope and ambition, seeking a mission. But he knew how to listen. Since then, I've written a few other books. (You can buy 'em. You can read 'em.) But this still feels like my first one. The papers turned into the book. Now you can buy it and read it. Period.

I enjoy examining that younger guy's wisdom. He's grown and changed, so there are some minor tweaks along the way, revising some thoughts and updating his language for more modern sensibilities. His parables and fables still hold up as examples of what the real world is like. To be honest, I expected reading this to be boring. These days when I read, I want stories—adventure, sci-fi, fantasy. I don't want to think; I want to escape! But I am grateful for and pleasantly surprised by what he has written.

Preface: In Retrospect

Some of his ideas have become common knowledge or sayings, but that only leads me to dig more into what he wrote!

I am starting to live through the things he imagined. My body is constantly reminding me of its weakness and frailty, though I still have strength. The control over parts of my life is limited, but I still have some say and most of my faculties. The younger man who wrote this book saw it coming, and his thoughts are helping me now.

When I was younger, my youth was often framed as inferiority. I resented the assumptions of older people who thought they had nothing to learn from their youngers. I am trying not to repeat that folly.

"Age brings wisdom," says the old fool. Sometimes people just get older.

Jesus of Nazareth was about 33 when he died, and a lot of people are still learning from him. The guy who wrote this book was younger than Jesus when he started it. Now I've lived longer than Jesus. And honestly, so what?

I'm happy that younger guy wrote what he did. I'm happy to put a little polish on it. I'm happy that in one way or another, I am that younger guy. I hope he helps you the way he helped me.

. . . or in your own way.

Prologue

The Bus Station

HELLO, FELLOW TRAVELER! YES, we are about to take our first steps together!

Before we get started, I'd like to tell you about one of my travels.

I was never a huge lottery player, but like many other things, I've dabbled in it. On my twentieth birthday, I bought a $20 scratch-off lottery ticket. Lo and behold, I won $200!

OK . . . I can hear you math wizzes already telling me that I only made $180 in the deal, but it was still a big win!

With my major award in hand, my girlfriend and I embarked on a Greyhound Bus for Philadelphia—her former stomping grounds. We spent the day tramping around Center City on foot, exploring old haunts and finding new nooks and crannies. For lunch, we found a classy little hole-in-the-wall with black-and-white blobs painted on the walls and enjoyed the only meal we could afford: an overpriced olive and cheese plate.

After a full day, we headed back to the Filbert Street Terminal (one of the busiest bus stations in the United States) to catch our reservation on the last ride home. A handful of people were already lined up, and more were gathering behind us, all with tickets in hand. Under the sterile halogen lights, an announcement came over the loudspeaker—our bus had been cancelled. A manager had mistakenly sent the driver home early and didn't feel like doing anything to correct it. My girlfriend and thirty of our newest companions just realized we were all stranded in the City of Brotherly Love.

At first, we all tried to get comfortable on the hard tile floors and held vigil into the night, taking turns to complain to the front desk that we all followed the rules and the schedule they posted. Word quickly spread that the bus line had a backup driver that they could call, and that company policy was to call in an extra bus if there were ten or more riders stranded. They never called. We had to wait until the first bus at 6:30 the next morning.

My girlfriend and I curled up in a doorway as the concrete room grew chilly and the roaches skittered between slim cracks of shade. Nobody was happy. Some grew angry.

We chatted with other travelers, who remained more pleasant despite their discomfort: the couple in the puffy jackets—his black, hers canary yellow; the grungy college kids heading home for break; the young family visiting relatives. One traveler, who some started to call "Princess," suffered in waves. She was part of our small circle in patient vigil, but every hour or so, she would become agitated and then call Daddy and loudly complain while he apologized on speakerphone. At some point in the night, Daddy consented to speed across the state. Just after 5:00 a.m., Daddy arrived and drove Princess home. The morning bus arrived early, and we were all boarded and rolling by 6:00 a.m.

This was a time of inconvenience, but we did not suffer. It was uncomfortable and unpleasant, but we were not in danger; we were not exposed to the elements. We were hungry, tired, and dirty, but we would recover fully in a day or so. It was hard to remind ourselves in the moment, but we were fine. We felt stranded, but there was a clear resolution before us: there was a bus coming for us, just later than we wanted.

Life is not necessarily suffering, but there is plenty of disquiet—reality failing to live up to our expectations. Buddhism describes this as the First Noble Truth. Common sense philosophers just say, "Life's a beast, and then you die."

Prologue

A week before the trip, my girlfriend and I had bought tickets for this night bus that never came. All day we had planned to get on it and be home that night. When we lined up in the station with those others, it was because we all expected that bus to be there. Life did not live up to any of our expectations. Some took it worse than others.

Someone wise once told me, "Wisdom is learning from other people's mistakes." I want to go with you on a journey that might have some wisdom along the way. Together we will travel to learn about life from Pharaoh, a figure whose villainy and downfall are recounted in the Exodus story of the Torah of Judaism, the Bible of Christianity, and the Qur'an of Islam. This is not a comparison or analysis of these revered religious texts but an examination of the character who is at the center of the story.

We will begin by looking at the very questions we ask. Part I of this book is a trek through the journalistic questions—a rethinking of the traditional "Five *W*s and an *H*." The very questions of Who, What, When, Where, Why, and How are broken down and reformed. Once we know what and how we are asking, we can examine the questions of suffering: What are we? Why do bad things happen do good people?

After we reach the summit—the truth behind the questions of suffering—we will continue to Part II, whence we will ask those questions of Pharaoh, the legendary villain who knew great power and great suffering. Then we will, as that wise person suggested, find what we can learn from his mistakes.

Together we will go, dear traveler. I am glad to go with you. Thanks for coming along!

Now let's get moving!

PART I: *Suffering Questions*

1
What Things

> All definitions are made in vain.
> – Ferdinand de Saussure, *Course in General Linguistics*

. . . And yet, we use words to talk about things. Before we talk about something, it helps to know what it is we are talking about. As we set out on this journey, we must think about what we are.

THE SALAD PROBLEM

Consider the salad. Take a moment and imagine one in your mind. What do you see? Are there croutons? Dressing on the side? What is a salad? And what makes it a salad?

A common image to come to mind: mixture of greens, sliced red onions, grape tomatoes, a sprinkle of cheese, hold the cucumbers please, all piled into a bowl with a dressing poured overtop. This common salad has its variations: the taco salad with tortillas and seasoned ground beef, the Pittsburgh salad with sliced steak and French fries on top, the Caesar with the anchovy dressing and Parmesan. These are slight variations on the theme of a mixture of lettuce with toppings and dressing. But that is not the only type of salad that exists.

Picnic salads are something altogether different. Ham salad, egg salad, potato salad, and macaroni salad hardly feature vegetables and don't have proper toppings. If these are included in our salad definition, then we must say that a salad is a mixture with some sort of dressing, which can be as thick as mayonnaise or thin as balsamic vinegar. This would work for the salads we have discussed so far.

But what about fruit salad and bean salad? There is not necessarily a proper dressing on those. I suppose one could argue that the fruit juice or bean juice is a dressing. But where is the dressing in a Jell-O salad? It is the gelatin? Including these examples in the definition of salad means that dressing cannot be a requirement. In that case, the definition of salad has been reduced to something that is an edible mixture.

The final turn of this circle of salads brings us back to the beginning. What if somebody prepares a bowl of plain lettuce with no toppings or dressing? That first common image would call that a salad, but it has no toppings, no dressing, and no mixture.

So what is a salad?

The only thing that all of the salads discussed above have in common is that they are edible. We already have a term for things that are edible: food. And I think we can agree that every food does not qualify as a salad.

While that question has entertained me far longer than I care to admit, it pushes the understanding of what makes a thing a thing. Philosophers, theologians, engineers, grilled-cheese enthusiasts, obnoxious people, and overthinkers have spent lifetimes thinking about what makes any given thing a thing. For some, it is an unseen core essence, a "saladness." For others, it is enough that we all simply agree to call these things salad.

SO CATEGORICAL

When we talk about something, it is important that we agree what it is. Spoken language is no more than grunts, and written language is no more than squiggly lines. To each of these, we try to attach ideas and hope that the people who hear our grunts or see our squiggles know what we mean. To communicate well, we rely on categories, or types of things.

An apple is famously different from an orange. It is also different from every other apple ever. Sure, every single one is unique, but it would be impossible for us to assign each apple a unique name. We need to speak of things in broad strokes. Our little brains need to lump similar things together and keep different things apart.

Oranges and apples are different types of fruits. An apple is not an orange and vice versa. If you compare individuals, yes, you will find differences. Generally speaking, an apple with an acidic tang is not a good thing. An orange that is green and red is usually not good to eat. However, oranges and apples are both fruits. In that way, their types can be compared—not to evaluate individuals within the type, but just for the sake of telling the difference between things.

We need categories to function. We need to know if what we are eating is potentially poisonous, or if a creature we are approaching could cause us harm. Basic survival depends on such simple categories.

There are multitudes of outraged armchair experts out there who boldly claim that using categories for anything is a bad thing. Unfortunately, that hard line ends up being less than helpful. First, because their rage is contagious. Second, because calling people simple, lazy, or small-minded for their use of such categories is a way of categorizing them, which is hypocritical.

But there is something that we can learn from these armchair experts. They seek to remove and reexamine outdated categories that have been overused. They want to move their language beyond the categories used by oppressive people who have used their power for harm. The armchair experts are heralds of the Post-Age—post-colonial, post-modern, post-Christian, post-category—where nothing is anything and everything is its own thing. While treating everything as unique is impossibly difficult, challenging harmful categories is as noble as it gets!

Everything is unique, and we should acknowledge that, yet we also need categories to make sense of how certain things tend to go together. We need to continually refine the way we think about things, and it is important to try to see that the world is full of beauty and diversity.

Old things can be smashed into their component parts, but we can't just leave the rubble. It is like a tower of building blocks in a room full of toddlers. It can be rebuilt, and it must be rebuilt. Sure, the new structures will be destroyed, but then they can be rebuilt again, hopefully even better.

Unbundling is a trend today. TV is the prime example. Individual channels and streaming services are breaking away from the lump subscriptions. Consumers can choose the content they like and ignore the rest. This unbundling is not only true in media content but also in relationships and religion. Choose the people you like, the prayers you like, and make it your own. Get rid of the rest.

But people also crave stability and commonality. We are stuck in our own competing struggles for uniqueness and belonging. Soon will come a time of rebundling. Custom bundling. We are building our own block towers, but we hope that we can still relate to others with them.

This unbundling and rebundling cycle is nothing new. It's just that now we have better technology than ever, so we can unbundle and rebundle more things. It will go on forever. Future generations will reject us as rigid and calcified, stuck in our ways, and out of touch. They will build their own block towers from the ruins of our bundles. They will have their own classifications, their own categories for things. This is what personalized algorithms are doing on an individual scale as we speak.

Associating one thing with another is not necessarily a problem. What matter is how people apply their categories.

Categories or types are descriptive. They are a shorthand to help us remember what we observe. We can use them to anticipate what other like things will be like but only to a limited extent.

What Things

A green apple will probably be tart. Then again, a category should not completely prescriptive; it does not make reality a certain way. If you encounter a green apple that is not tart, then so be it. You learned something. There is an important difference between saying "all green apples are tart" and "I observe that green apples tend to be tart." When you realize that not every green apple is tart, the world becomes bigger, more colorful, and more flavorful.

Usually when you are hungry for an apple, you just want an apple. Maybe you like it sweeter. Maybe you like it sour. But when you imagine wanting an apple, your mind will not conjure an image of a specific apple (unless you have one set aside). You just want an apple. Crunch!

THE HUMAN THING

There is this type of thing called a human. I am told that I am one of them and don't really take issue with that.

The question of what makes a human is a big problem, because humans want to be special. That goes for us as individuals but also as a species. Humans want to be above nature, transcendent, more than mere animals. Religious and nonreligious alike have looked for all sorts of reason why we as a species are special. Here we will look first at what we are made of, then what about that may or may not be transcendent.

If you are not human and you are reading this, I would very much like to talk to you. I'm sorry if I misspeak and offend you with any of these meditations. Like everyone, I'm only working with what I think I know.

The human is made up of three selves—the selves of body, mind, and spirit. These selves of the human overlap and intertwine. If one part is removed, there is no human, no life, no being. These interact but are inseparable: body, mind, and spirit.

The body is the most obvious part. It is the tangible, concrete mass—the physical self. It is the facet of the human most affected by physical forces. Gravity holds us to the planet. The body can sense when it bumps into another physical thing. Defining the body requires little explanation because we can easily observe it using our own body's senses.

The mind is less visible, but there is little debate over whether it exists. The mind formulates ideas, defines categories, and renders judgments. It is the mental self. It is tied into the body through the brain and the rest of the nervous system. The body's senses take inputs and send them into the brain. It is clear that the mind and body are inextricably connected. Without the mind, the body cannot move itself. Without the body, the mind is alone, unable to sense or express itself.

The spirit is the most difficult to define. History has attached many meanings to what the spirit can be. For the sake of our conversation, we will stick with the observable concept. If you prefer to attach more transcendental or religious meaning, I will leave room for you to do so. I will not exclude the more transcendent view, but there is a basic understanding of spirit that lies beneath.

Spirit is the intangible self. It is the influence that you have on the world. Like the wind, it is not visible in itself, but it can be seen in the things that it touches. It is expressed in your actions and creations. It is what touches other things and people. The spirit's effects are not always immediately felt.

For example, you are reading this book. I have long finished writing it and quite possibly forgotten most of its content. Yet part of me is influencing you—my spirit lives through this. If it impacts your thoughts or feelings, however slightly, then my spirit is connecting with yours.

The impact of spirit tends to weaken over time. Voices and thoughts recede as others grow to prominence. Memories fade. Spirits are lost.

Thinking this way about spirit is not magical; it merely acknowledges that our actions have an impact on the world. You have an intangible self that is at play beyond your body and mind. Branches of your being are dancing through the world. If you walk into somebody and scowl or smile, that will impact their body immediately and their mind for a while after. You continue to touch their spirit long after the physical contact.

The spirit is real.

(Sometimes people talk of similar ideas using the terms "heart and soul," but this is not the place for that type of discussion. Those are mystical or religious categories that often overlap with the spirit. The heart is a pump for blood in your chest, and the soul is a religious idea that is not shared by everybody and originally merely meant "life." In some cases, spirit is a synonym for either or both of those. Let's not get hung up on these. For our purposes here, we can keep it simple.)

ISN'T THAT SPECIAL

A human is not the only thing with a physical self. A rock has a body in the broadest sense. Animate or inanimate objects alike have a physical self. Rocks do not have minds but birds do. Most animals are capable of categorizing things as safe or dangerous, food or poison, and make decisions as to what they will do next.

Using the basic sense of spirit, animals have one as well. Their influence can be felt after their actions. People have memories of their pet dogs. Their dogs rarely leave behind memoirs to read about and have later influence, but the animals have lasting influence nonetheless.

But can an inanimate object have a lasting influence on a person's behavior? Does it have a spirit of its own? The answer might seem obvious, but it is complicated.

Consider a freshly baked brownie. It has a physical presence. It also gives off an aroma, which is a physical expression. That delicious smell reaches your nostrils, and suddenly, the brownie has an influence on you. Even as I write this, the imaginary brownie that I am writing about is making my mouth water and my stomach growl. That imaginary brownie spirit does not even have a body!

Does the brownie have some rudimentary spirit that touched me, or was my mind just imagining that? Was I projecting myself onto something inanimate, or does every bit of matter hold some intangible sway over the rest? The universe is a very connected place. I suggest you consult at least one brownie before coming to a conclusion on this.

(If you dislike brownies, it is still impacting you by causing mild revulsion. Please find a friend to share your brownies with rather than wasting them.)

But other examples show this connection. A warrior views their weapon as an extension of themselves; their spirit extends into the object. The Rifleman's Creed of a United States Marine codifies this connection between warrior and weapon: "My rifle is human, even as I, because it is my life. Thus, I will learn it as a brother...We will become part of each other..."[1]

Even the average car driver allows colored lines of paint and light signals to determine their behaviors and boundaries. Stop here. Go now. Stay on this side. Proceed with caution.

So what is special about the human? Many things have bodies, minds, and spirits, so what is it? Is the body more dexterous? Is the mind more capable? Is the spirit stronger?

The answers are mixed.

The human body is not the only one with nimble thumbs, or hair, or an upright posture. It does not have the best individual features, but it is unique in its combination of those.

The human mind is not the only one that can communicate, remember, feel, or decide. It is not the best at all of those but is unique in its combination of capabilities.

The human spirit reaches out and touches and is also touched. It is not the only influence in the world, but it is unique in its way. The human spirit can be aware of its influence on outside things.

SPECTERS AND THE SIMPLE SAGE

Each of these human facets—the body, mind, and spirit—have hungers, fervors, and the need for rest. The hungers of the body

---

1. "Marine's Rifle Creed." United States Marine Corps History Division. https://www.usmcu.edu/Research/Marine-Corps-History-Division/Frequently-Requested-Topics/Marines-Rifle-Creed.

What Things

are simply called hungers. The hungers of the mind are curiosities. The hunger of the spirit is to be engaged with the spirit of another in community. When these hungers are not fed, that part of you grows weak. When they are overfed, that part of you can take over and throw the whole self out of balance.

A fervor is the desire to act, create, and reach in a particular way. For the body, the fervors are movements. For the mind, the fervor is contemplation. For the spirit, the fervor is to reach out and touch another. Like hungers, fervors must be mediated and kept in balance. Overreaching fervors can lead to weakness or foolishness.

Rest is the type of action that is repressed the most by ambitious fervors. The body, mind, and spirit can be fueled and pushed, but if they are not allowed to rest in between these cycles, they will break down. The body must be still. The mind must sleep. The spirit must center itself.

When the hungers, fervors, and rest begin to fall out of balance, a human begins to veer into certain traps. At times, intervention can be necessary. Medicines and therapies of all sorts—mental, physical, and spiritual can help bring a person back into balance.

People sometimes need help to keep them in balance. There are countless mental, physical, and spiritual conditions that require great attention and continuous intervention to help a person keep this balance and maintain their human dignity. With our three selves needing maintenance, it can become difficult to sustain balance, and the person can become influenced by a specter—a monstrous ghoul that makes one self take over the others.

The specter called the Brute causes the body to take over. The Brute makes it so that the body's cravings drive everything. Whether they hunger for food or sex or exercise or luxury, too many of any of these things will lead down foolish paths. The Brute possesses a person to only follow physical impulses, living an empty life of chasing pleasure after pleasure, looking for happiness but finding emptiness. The Brute does not control every gym rat, barfly, or twitterpated bunny, but such people can be vulnerable to the Brute.

The Curse of Pharaoh

The specter called the Cypher makes the mind take over. The body and spirit are left to deteriorate. One possessed by the Cypher grows physically weak and spiritually isolated. The Cypher might make a person learn very much or become very skillful in mind, but eventually the person prefers accuracy over relationship, conclusion over kindness, judgment over mercy. A Cypher makes someone unapproachable, unable to communicate with others because it does not tend to its body or spirit. I know many who have fallen to Cyphers, who have become less and less able to hold a normal conversation. They correct people for not being precise enough and will often employ the term "technically" when they do it. I grow sad for their isolation, with only the Cypher and themselves. The Cypher does not mind.

The specter of the Tyrant makes the spirit takes over. The Tyrant wants to exercise influence over others. One possessed by the Tyrant must be in constant motion, interacting with people or things, exerting itself all around. The Tyrant is perpetually agitated and drives its host to madness. The Tyrant is driven by a paradox: it wants to have power over others, but it becomes increasingly dependent on the people it tries to control. Then a specter of a Tyrant takes a person over; they cannot rest; they lose self-awareness; they grow as sick as their body; their mind falls to pieces. A Tyrant can take over any type of person. Politics are an obvious orchard of people possessed by Tyrant specters; that is almost too easy to state. Tyrants are far more prevalent than that. A Tyrant drives any person to control others—manipulating, micromanaging, throwing fits when things do not go their way.

But balance between our internal selves is necessary to fight off these specters and fully experience joy. A person who aims their mind, body, and spirit in balance will make mistakes, will morph and recover, and will find ways to adapt. It is this person who I call the simple sage.

A simple sage is wise in their quest and maintenance of boundaries and balance. The simple sage feeds, exercises, and rests their mind, body, and spirit to the best of their ability.

There are simple sages out in the world, simply living their lives. They do not seek attention, fame, or success, but they are worthy of admiration—perhaps more than any famous saint or hero.

BEING HUMAN

Humanity is the type of something that you and I (probably) have in common. We can debate what exactly that thing is that we have in common. Here I present that a human is three unique selves —the body, mind, and spirit—each of which has different capabilities and capacities than any other species. To live fully and enjoy this humanity to its utmost, a balance must be struck by mediating hungers, fervors, and rest. The simple sage avoids the imbalance of specters in order to fully embrace its humanity.

But a human does not live in isolation. A human touches the world with their body and spirit. A human interacts with other humans, other species, and other things in the outside world. You are not simply you. I am not simply me. Whatever it is that connects us, together we are.

We are travelers through life; that we are. And this particular we—you, me, and anyone else who might be reading along—are sharing this little bit of our journey. Welcome, fellow traveler, as we continue toward deeper questions. On we go!

2

The Ways of Whence

> There are three things that matter in real estate:
> location, location, location. – Lord Harold Samuel

WELL, WHAT WAS GOING on in that first chapter? What is the point of "the What"? Where does it fit in with everything else? When is it going to make sense? Are we going to get to the story . . . or at least the main point of this book some time soon?

We'll get there by following along this little bit of life's road together. Fellow traveler, Whence is the name of the roads we travel in life.

The question of Whence is the question of context. It is the arrangement of several Whats—their proximity to each other, their order, their interactions. Whence is commonly, and appropriately, split into the Where and the When. These two take slightly different approaches to the question of context, arranging the Whats in space or time.

THE FUNNIEST JOKE EVER TOLD

There is a legendary account of the Greek philosopher Chrysippus, who lived about 2,300 years ago. As it goes, he saw a donkey who had broken free and got into a store of figs. When another

The Ways of Whence

bystander asked him what to do, he replied, "Give it some wine to wash them down!" Chrysippus, in the bliss of his magnificent joke, laughed himself to death.

What do you think? Was it that funny?

What if I told you that figs were extremely expensive and that the wine he suggested drinking was equally expensive? Also, donkeys back then were viewed as the same stubborn asses that many people consider them today.

A modern (and fictional) version of the events might help out. Let's give it a try:

A baboon broke free from the zoo and broke into a five-star sushi restaurant. It found the most exotic cuts of rare fish and started chowing down. The owner found the scene and called the police, saying, "what should I do? This baboon is eating the finest fish in the city!" The police dispatcher answered, "Offer it a bottle of your best sake!"

Is that any better? Is it an example that suits a context you can connect with? I gather that, no matter what the context, it is far more difficult to laugh at a joke when somebody tells you how funny it will be.

Humor needs context. For a joke to work, the person hearing the joke has to understand the elements you're talking about and has to agree with whatever unexpected twist you work in.

These days some comedians can be heard griping about how "you can't make jokes about anything anymore!" That gripe is often part of a conversation about changing understandings of what is offensive and inappropriate. As time goes on, more people become aware of how harmful some ideas are—despite their former widespread use. I see humorous new things every day about all sorts of things. Comedians who complain about being offensive don't realize that they are just not funny.

Comedy is hard—and always has been.

THE THREE ROADS

To understand the first part of Whence—the Where—we will look at the roads we walk or roll through in life. This ramble is not based on physical ability but instead reflects the metaphorical paths traveled throughout a lifetime.

Every step we take lands on more than one road because the road of life is three roads in one. And each movement is more than your body moving forward. It causes motion that goes far beyond what you can sense.

The Personal Road

The first road is the road you know best. It is the Personal Road. The Personal Road is composed of that which is immediately around you. It is the clothing on your skin, the rocks beneath your feet, the air around your body. This is the road in which you can see the most immediate impact of your actions. This is the world that you touch, see, or otherwise sense most fully.

Your relationships in the Personal Road are the people that you know best. You can anticipate many responses from this environment. They are friends, family, lovers, enemies, coworkers, and others that you spend the most time with or near. You know their names, their habits, their lives.

The Personal Road is the one that people tend to care the most about. It is immediate and gives us feedback quickly. If we kick it, it kicks back. If we hug it, we will feel the warmth of love.

Though a person cannot perfectly anticipate even their own action, the things that happen within the Personal Road are the most predictable. However, when these actions take unexpected turns, they can bring the deepest sort of pain.

Your immediate road is part of another, bigger road. Beyond the Personal Road is the Local Road, which is part of a bigger world. It is the place where many Personal Roads overlap and interact. Other Personal Roads will interact with your road, and your influence impacts the roads of others.

Sometimes we encounter an unfamiliar road, and sometimes others encounter us unexpectedly. Perhaps you hold the door for somebody at the coffee shop—somebody you will never see again. You have directly encountered another person but will probably never again be a part of their Personal Road. If you learn their name, you are likely to forget it soon. People along your Local Road are sometimes better remembered by their roles. This is not because you are rude or callous but because the human brain is a limited resource.

Even though you might not know your barista's birthday, a simple sage will remember that every barista is a person with a birthday.

The spirit of your actions will impact those who you see, even if you think that you are insignificant. Even though our limited brains cannot see all the moving parts of the world, your being is important and influential.

The Local Road

The Local Road is the next layer. It has a wide range and involves many types of relationships, both seen and hidden. I do not know the person who made my shoes because they live in a country on a continent far away. Yet the fruit of their labor allows me to tread through mud and stones. The Local Road also includes many people that you know but not especially well. Friends, extended family, peers, colleagues, acquaintances, regulars, and "oh, I think I met them at that birthday party last year" share your Local Road.

The Cosmic Road

Beyond the Local Road is the Cosmic Road. It is the road that is most difficult to influence for an individual. Instead, the Cosmic Road's influence on people is almost entirely one-way. Consider the sun. It provides heat for the planet and food for photosynthetic plants. It burns your skin if you stay out too long. It hurts your eyes even if you look at it for a mere second. Most people and animals build their daily schedule around its appearance in the sky. And yet at this point, there is nothing that humans have done to majorly influence the sun. We cannot move it or darken it. Despite our advances in nuclear technology, our most devastating bombs are nothing but a spark to the solar inferno.

Of course, there are countless stars beyond our own. Perhaps our reach will grow with technology, but even so, our impact on even our solar system is minimal. We are absurdly tiny. The Cosmic Road is made up of countless Local Roads and Personal Roads. It is Cosmic because we will not directly interact with all of it.

The Personal, Local, and Cosmic Roads are permeable to a degree. Things and people transition in and out of them as time goes on. For example, a regular at a diner and a server who become friends transition from the Local Road into each other's Personal Roads. Coworkers also can move through these boundaries. In fact, a close friend is a person who was previously outside of the Personal Road but enters it. The same is true for people who travel, briefly inserting themselves into Local Roads far away before returning to their home; sometimes the traveler will make friends, impacting a Personal Road far from their own locality.

Similarly, those who fall out of acquaintance leave the Personal Road. Consider the grade-school friends who share a daily lunch table. So many disappear as years pass. Some may stay close, but many fade into their own distant lives.

These roads are important to people because different types of relationships help define us further. Relationship names are signals of what people are near you. A father has a child. An aunt has a sibling who has children. A friend has someone who wants to be near them. These roles all belong to the Personal Road.

In the Local Road, the relationships become less personal and more transactional; they rely on exchange, value, or usefulness. Bosses have employees. Patrons have servers. Professionals have clients. Celebrities have fans. Politicians have constituents. When we observe people who only belong to our province, we tend to know them more based on their roles and traits rather than their character.

Our relationships in the Cosmic Road are far more singular and radically equal. Yet our views tend to oversimplify, using those imperfect categories we discussed in "the What." We build our understanding of things and people beyond our Local Road by grouping them with our limited knowledge. We speak of entire groups with shorthand phrases, often associating them with one or two broad characteristics. It is very easy for our generalizations to become confused and skewed. We can speak of distant humans unfavorably—and even as though they are not human at all.

Our tiny brains and limited lifespans do not allow us to get to know every individual, but that is not an excuse to forget that others are humans just like us. We cannot forget that our generalizations are—at best—partial pictures. At their worst, generalizations can lead us to see others as a few limited features rather than people.

The same is true in our relationship with things. Just because something is different or distant, it does not mean that it is unimportant. The Cosmic can become Personal. A cataclysm on a distant corner of the globe can very quickly impact your present life.

The cosmos is small. Like our humanity, it is something that we hold in common. Whether we are astral accidents or self-moving space dust, we are children of this universe. Perhaps we are even children of something beyond the universe. Whatever the human's relationship to the cosmos, it is the same among all of us. And we are very, very small.

JUST IN TIME—BEFORE, DURING, AND AFTER

As with space, time also has three moments from our perspective. These are before, during, and after. All events are compared to other events. What is before gives meaning to what is during and what that happens after. The phrase "wrong place at the wrong time" and its variants are simply commentary on context, the Whence. Crossing the road is a simple example: if your timing is right, then you and a motor vehicle will not attempt to occupy the same space at the same time.

Context can be frustrating because in many situations, we don't always know what comes before. Nor do we know what will come after. Nor do we know all of the relationships of the people and things we interact with. It is impossible to understand and account for everything, yet we try, and the effort is meaningful. Thinkers, storytellers, jokesters, writers, and many others seek to create things that are broadly applicable and appealing. Such efforts are impossible but nonetheless noble. Just as everything we encounter has its own context, so do we. Every person has their own influences and aims.

I have had many conversations with elders from prior generations who will often use terms that are unintentionally derogatory or harmful. They were raised in a context where such language was commonplace and did not realize the harm that it caused or the hate that created it. They did not create the hate; they did not intend the harm. They might have never encountered a person who would be harmed by it on their Personal Road or Local Road. This language is almost always connected to race, sexuality, or mental and physical ability. When possible, I try to explain the harm of those terms. There is a common reaction: "That used to be OK. I guess you can't say anything anymore."

They are speaking from a place of frustration because the language they are most familiar with is being questioned. The fact is, derogatory terms were always harmful and never should have been used. They were never OK. It just so happened that they were not walking Local Roads with people who could show them the harm of those terms. Either that or they did not care to imagine the harm those words cause.

ETHICS AND CONTEXT

The roads and moments of context make actions meaningful. The command to kill every rodent you see means something different to an exterminator or a zookeeper. A person having their stomach slashed open can be horrific if they are in a park out for a jog but heroic if they are in a hospital with a surgeon. Context adds dimension, adds thickness, adds meaning to every action and interaction that we do. We can never understand the full extent of even a single action.

It is also impossible not to offend or unfavorably interact with someone or something along the line. Even concepts of offense and humor differ in diverse contexts. There are many things other than jokes that will impact the roads of others for better and worse, and the miniscule cascading of events—the butterfly effect—shows this.

Could a butterfly's wings eventually lead to a hurricane? It's hard to tell, and that's the point. Humans are much closer to each other than we realize. We metaphorically and literally bump into others all the time. These encounters are sometimes trivial but always influential.

Many who study ethics will not avoid the opportunity to complain about people treating ethics as contextual. They tend to prefer ideas of universal mandates or ideals of virtue. Ethics may or may not be based on universal truths, but they are always applied in a context that is far more complicated than one can anticipate.

It is also true that people perceive good and evil differently. Ethicists might argue about what is correct and mistaken, who is good or evil. Outside of their debates, one cannot deny that—regardless of who might be correct—there are different perspectives. The old quip that "one person's terrorist is another's freedom fighter," though cliché, exemplifies this. A terrorist is one who attempts to inspire public fear for their aims. A freedom fighter serves as an example to help free the oppressed. Regardless of ultimate ideals, any person who uses violence against a power and toward their aims can hardly avoid being viewed as both good and evil.

So what is right? What should we do? We do not move through time haphazardly. We make choices in all sorts of context. The events before and after, and the people on all roads, are connected.

CONVERGING ROADS

This moment on this little bit of road is our time together. I will not propose that we will solve everything on this short journey, but I do hope that it leads us somewhere new—somewhere where we can understand in a way that we could not before. On we go! Now we must find out how we will travel this little stretch of road together.

3

The Steps of How

> If you see a turtle on a fence post,
> you know it didn't get there by itself.
> – An old saying from the Southern United States

HERE AND NOW, WE encounter How. How is a connector, the question that links events through time. It is the question of processes and methods, of order and systems. How something happened, or came to be, requires the What and the Whence. What is it? What was it? Whence does it exist now? The How is the line that connects the dots.

The How will be our directions on this little stretch or road. How will be our navigation, our sequence, our step-by-step.

MR. FINE'S PINES

Mr. Fine was a friendly man, well-loved in his community. There was a comfortable and familiar air around him, a friendly wit and cheerful banter that connected him to everyone he met. Many people around town gladly claimed him as one like a father, uncle, or grandfather.

Mr. Fine loved them too.

As a way of showing his love, Mr. Fine befriended the masons, handymen, woodworkers, and carpenters around town and took their scraps back to his own woodshop. Late into the nights he would work with hunks and chunks, tattered, angled, and broken pieces of every type and stain. Mr. Fine smoothed the sharp edges, formed the obscure, and connected the disparate bits into meaningful little handiworks.

Cars with spinning wheels, spotted dogs, whimsical hobbyhorses for frolicking in yards, and boats to float down the creeks. He made every imaginable toy and curio to give to the children, and they loved him all the more.

This is a pleasant story, though it does not end there.

Over time, the children treasured their toys—not by preserving them as mantelpieces but by using them as the playthings they were. Axles fell apart, spots faded, horses lost their mane, boats drifted away.

As the children grew, the toys broke.

When Mr. Fine took his final rest, the children gathered and shared their memories, their stories of the toys. Those things had been made with love. Those reminders accompanied them through their gleeful youth.

Those things were made from rubbish.

Those things became rubbish.

They shared the fate of all things, including Mr. Fine himself. Their lives were lost.

As inevitable as death is, it does make a difference what happens in between.

If those scraps had gone straight into the dump, nobody would have known the difference. But Mr. Fine delayed those scraps turning into trash and made them into something new. They still ended up in the trash eventually, but first they changed people's lives.

Everything ends up garbage eventually, but it makes a difference how it gets that way.

SO RANDOM

"Purple banana ice cream ninjas!" was the working title of this section because it seemed random and quirky. On the day that phrase popped into my head, I looked around and considered my surroundings. A large, purple vase held flowers in the corner of my apartment's living room. I had eaten a banana with breakfast, and the peel was on top of the compost bowl. It was hot, and I wanted something cool and sweet; ice cream would be nice. My karate bag sat across the room, with nunchucks and a bamboo sword sitting next to it, so we get ninjas.

I wanted to come up with phrase that was spontaneous and random. But despite my best efforts, every last bit of it could be explained.

The term "random" has come into major disuse. People want to seem interesting and unpredictable. They hate the idea that they are boring, common, ordinary, basic. Random has come to mean something more like "exciting."

The fact is that nothing is random. Nothing spontaneously appears without origin. Certainly every moment is novel, and at times unexpected, but everything that happens is a consequence of what has come before it.

This is not to say that we do not have some control over the future. The universe is not determined. Our actions have consequences that are not yet determined. But these are not random. These are at best unexpected.

SCIENTIFIC

The question of How is inquiring about a sequence of events. How has this come to be? What has come before that has led to this? How did the turtle get onto the fence post? How did this seemingly random phrase pop into my head?

When the How is answered, its ideas can be transposed onto other processes. How can we do this again? Is this really the How that caused this event?

This is the work of science. Science looks for connections between processes and their outcomes and tries to find the fine threads that connect events. Unfortunately, the world is quite messy. There are so many forces and spirits floating and interacting that it is often a great challenge to distill what exactly is causing one thing or another.

As humans, we naturally try to connect events that happen to us. As individuals, we have a very limited perspective and only very few experiences, but we try our best to connect the events in our lives and learn from them in order to better anticipate and deal with new events as they come along. When dark clouds roll into the sky, you probably want to go inside and close all of your windows. When light flashes from those clouds, you prepare for the roar of thunder.

Science is the concerted effort to compile many events from many people and standardize the explanations. Imagine a person who regularly does yard work, and when they finish, a storm always follows. Without any outside information, it would be reasonable for that person to assume that their yard work somehow causes the dark clouds and everything that follows.

By taking many stories, guessing trends, and testing them in experiments many times, the truths about the world can be distilled. The scientific method observes the world, forms a hypothesis, tests the hypothesis, observes the outcomes, forms a new hypothesis, and on and on it goes.

For decades there has been a campaign to malign science and its findings. This is usually directed by people who do not like what the science finds and relies on people who do not understand how science finds things. Science is a process that aims to continually improve itself. Of course, science has made mistakes, but with new and better information, science corrects itself.

When someone has an experience different from the general findings of science, it does not mean that the science is wrong. Science often accounts for variations. Science tells you what tends to happen.

Science is not the creation of facts but the careful uncovering of them. A scientist is anyone who tries something many times and many ways in order to find out how it usually works. Scientific facts, laws, and theories are not merely asserted; they are tested, critiqued, refined, and corrected. True science is open to its failures, because the aim of learning is more important than maintaining refuted truths.

ARTSY

Science is a fickle discipline. It is unquestionably valuable.

But there is a trap that champions of science can stumble into: sometimes they overstate its power, especially when they imagine science as the ruler or enemy of other ways of knowing the world, such as religion and art.

Art is the twin to science—a mirror image. But what is the difference?

Is it the presence of a method? Art has highly refined techniques and methods for countless media forms.

Is it the aim for truth? Art has its own way of accessing the truth.

Is the difference repetition versus uniqueness? Is science made up of repeated experiments, while art is made up of unique experiences? The problem here is that science is constantly innovating and therefore unique, while repetition is present in art—such as recurring themes in music or the visual duplications of pop art.

So is there any difference between art and science?

Rather than separating the two, I think that the difference is more subtle. The difference is not what one has and the other does not. Instead, it is a matter of emphasis. Art prefers to create—be it beauty or a response from those who experience it. Science prefers to discover—trends, principles, and undiscovered facets of reality.

Science certainly creates too: every experiment is something new, an invention of the scientist; it can also evoke strong responses. "Eureka! I've found it!" is the cry of one who has experienced something new. Art definitely discovers; it unlocks truths of humanity, experience, and life itself. Both are full of discipline and improvisation, classic conventions and new trends.

The sibling rivalry of these vast enterprises will continue, but as with most siblings, the differences between them are largely exaggerated.

KNOWLEDGE AND INTELLIGENCE

Despite their rivalry, neither art nor science gives a person an advantage in intelligence. Intelligence is something that students of science like to claim as their own, but simply preferring science over art means nothing.

"How could you not know that?!" is a refrain proudly trumpeted by one who has forgotten that they did not always know the things that they know. It is easy to become sophomoric: a combination of the Greek terms *sophos*, which means "wisdom," and *moros*, which means "fool" (and is the source of the word "moron"). A sophomore is a person who has learned something of value that changes their worldview, though they do not necessarily understand its complexities. That is why the term is applied to second-year students in higher education—ones who know slightly more than when they were merely freshmen. Because their new information has quickly become integral to their existence, they begin to wonder how another person could function without it.

The sophomore fallacy emerges, in which people believe that the world would be better if everybody else would realize what they know. The fallacy is that others have the energy, intelligence, ability, or desire to understand and apply such changes to make the world better. When hungry people are gathered for a picnic, few will ponder what makes a salad a salad.

I have met countless students across academic and practical disciplines who say things like "if only they had better training . . ." or "if only they understood that . . ." It is a heartbreaking reality that many people either cannot understand or do not care to make changes. People have limited energies, abilities, and time

The Steps of How

and find security in doing things in imperfect but familiar ways. Unfortunately, in most situations for most people, comfort defeats correction. This does not mean that truth and innovation have no value; it means that the task of sharing knowledge is riddled with challenges.

So: "How could you not know that?" Those who say such things often fail to realize that the other person might not be interested or might not require such facts. "How could you not know the directions to your nearest lumber outlet?" "How could you not know the freezing point of saltwater?" "How could you not know that Smash Mouth's song 'I'm a Believer' from the *Shrek* movies was written by Neil Diamond? Wait . . . you don't know who Neil Diamond is?"

I have unscientifically observed that those who study sciences tend to assert that they know more about everything else. Not only is this a dubious claim, but it is also a rude one. There is value in the scientific method and the knowledge derived from its use, but liking science does not automatically grant intellectual superiority. Regardless of what exactly is known, this demonstrates a fundamental confusion about the difference between intelligence and knowledge.

Knowledge is the collection of information, facts, and experiences that are gathered and accessible for a person at a given time. Knowledge is the sum of building blocks or puzzle pieces.

Intelligence is the way those building blocks and puzzle pieces are used. Intelligence is taking what is known and seen and making sense of it. Sometimes people need more puzzle pieces to see the entire image. Sometimes people are able to reconfigure the pieces and make a new image.

Knowledge is the What. Intelligence is the How. Modern technological advances show this difference so well. In the age of artificial intelligence (AI), it is clear that these AIs have access to troves of knowledge, but their challenge is reconfiguring knowledge in a way that is useful or meaningful.

There are many types of intelligence, many ways to assemble the blocks of knowledge that we carry around. And knowing a certain set of facts does not make one person (or thing) more intelligent than another.

LEGS: THE COUNCIL OF REASON

The How is about connections and processes. Reasoning is the process of the mind, the exercise of intelligence. In the human, there are four voices that influence this exercise. This "Council of Reason" wrangles and debates within each person over the best conclusions. Information enters through the senses, and the voices on the council—Logic, Emotion, Gut, and Sophia—all vie for their preferred course of action.

Logic

Logic is the clearest connector of reason. It sequences and orders information to process it. Logic is often conflated with reason itself, but that is not fair to either one. The voice called Logic is connected to deductive reasoning—when conclusions can be made based on available general knowledge. For example, it takes an hour to make this casserole. It is 5:00 p.m. Dinner will be ready (but still hot!) at 6:00 p.m. Dinnertime, in this case, can be inferred from a clear sequence of predictable, known facts.

There is very much in the universe that does not follow this sort of Logic. Existence itself is a challenge to Logic as we understand it. What is simply *is*. Personally, I cannot fathom how an ordered universe would allow something as volatile as life to last for very long—especially the absurd and perverse life-form that we call humanity. Yet here we are!

Emotion

Emotion is often critiqued as going against Logic or reasoning as a whole, but that is simply not the case. Loyalty and dedication are functions of emotion. These do not merely help us maintain relationships with people but also with information. If a person has held something as true for a long time, they are likely to give that information more weight when arguments are levied against it. Emotion determines which facts are prioritized and which are held closest. This is how people can be repeatedly shown that something they believe is not true but still maintain that belief.

Emotion also is fascinating because it connects facts and events in ways that Logic cannot. Emotion takes disconnected pieces of information and transforms them into stories. It can make leaps where Logic only sees gaps. This voice called Emotion is connected to inductive reasoning—when we have limited examples or incomplete information to inform our conclusions. Conclusions from emotion can be creative, intuitive, and innovative.

Such leaps can offer great insight, but they can also create false realities. If I am trying to schedule dinner but have never made the casserole before, I cannot be sure how long it will really take. The recipe says one hour, but sometimes recipes don't account for enough time to chop up the vegetables! Let's call it an hour and a half; dinner will be at 6:30 p.m.

Gut

Gut reacts. Somewhere in our depths, in the realm of instinct, we are able to make instantaneous decisions with no discernible thought. Acting upon reflex or impulse can be especially useful when time is short. If you see a person tripping next to you, it will not help them if you sit down and write a pro-con list about the benefits of helping them. Either your arms reach out to help them stabilize, or you watch them fall on their face. This voice is connected to abductive reasoning—which requires us to decide and act with very limited information and time.

Back to that dinnertime scenario: it's 5:00 p.m. I don't know how long this new casserole will take, and everyone is going to be hungry soon. I'm just going to heat up a frozen pizza and try the casserole another time. Decision made.

While Gut is ideal in urgent situations, it is helpful to check it against the rest of the Council when time permits. Sometimes the Gut can assess better than the best Logic and most insightful Emotion, but other times its conclusions are too quick to be anything but slipshod.

Sophia

Sophia, the name of Wisdom (and derived from *sophos*), is the most evasive member of the council. If reasoning can be compared to creating images from limited pieces, then Sophia is the frame. Sophia understands where particular conclusions fit in a grander scheme. It sees beyond the particulars of one decision, instead viewing life and its decisions in the cosmic context. Wisdom weighs its choices not only against prior decisions of the individual who is reasoning but from external experiences that it has learned. Wisdom is not always apparently logical, but it works on a larger scale, considering possible outcomes over time and the deeper values at play in getting to those outcomes.

With one last visit to this dinnertime scenario, Sophia will voice other considerations about the casserole and the pizza, even after the choice has been made. The frozen pizza might not achieve the same nutritional goals or sense of personal accomplishment as the casserole, but maybe the alternative has its own unique benefits. The pizza will be out of the oven by 5:15 p.m., and the extra time will allow for games or activities to build special memories and stronger relationships. Perhaps some other time we can make the casserole together.

Together, the Council of Reason—Logic, Emotion, Gut, and Sophia—wrangle and work to help you make good decisions. Logic can be meticulous in following potential paths. Emotion cares about relationships and narratives, which helps it benefit both the individual and their community. Gut gets things done when they are imperative. Sophia considers possibilities on a transcendent scale. Of course, you govern who wins out in a given situation, whose decision you will follow.

The Steps of How

It is no good to rely on only one of these. None are universally better than the other. Logic carries based on what facts are available and is subject to deception. Emotion differs and can dismiss pertinent information and rely on assumptions. Gut has a limited scope and ignores what is not immediately apparent. Sophia tends to be narrower and less universal than it cares to admit.

None of these are perfect. Every person's reasoning is imperfect, incomplete.

Intelligence and reasoning are not exclusive to humans. Bees communicate the location of flowers through interpretive dance—connecting ideas to motion and interpreting symbolic gestures. Amazonian mice can fall from the canopy and navigate the underbrush for miles, even if they have never been in it before. Try that without a GPS!

INFINITE HOWS

The world is full of countless processes, not only within the minds of beings but in every imaginable way. Growth, life, death, decomposition, thought, invention, creation, destruction. All of these are answers to the question How.

And we humans are continually undergoing processes. Not only is the mind reasoning, but the body is in constant flux, perpetual becoming—cell by cell, atom by atom, thought by thought.

The spirit is perpetually becoming.

That might sound like a religious statement, but religion, spirituality, and other things of that sort do not seek to answer How. They are not focused solely on processes. They belong to a different question altogether.

My dear fellow traveler, our directions are about to take us past dangerous cliffs, but it is the best way to reach our summit. It is time to move towards that ultimate question. But along the way, there is something else we must navigate—and quickly!

4

The Cliffs of Why

Leisure is the mother of philosophy. – Thomas Hobbes

Why?... Why?... Why?... – A brooding college student or an average three-year-old

A WORD OF WARNING, my fellow traveler: beware! We must pass quickly across this treacherous terrain. It is necessary, but it is dangerous and has been the fall of many. The cliffs of Why are full of loose rocks and steep drops. We must quickly make sense of it and move on. We can do this! We must not stay for long!

OUT OF THE MOUTHS OF BABES

The pristine mind of children is an amazing mirror for what we once were, and for what we wish to become. When we listen to their observations, we see the world in a way that we have forgotten. They have a primordial insight because their world is bound by simple rules. We call them brilliant because they are simple.

As we grow, we spend so much time trying to make the universe seem simple, but the more we try, the more difficult it becomes.

Children demand explanations constantly. Why, they ask, is the sky blue? Why is the grass green? Why is the moon in the sky?

Why are birds scared of people? Your best answer only makes way for another Why, and another.

Parents, teachers, babysitters, siblings, and friends can become easily frustrated with the onslaught of Whys. I suspect that they suddenly realize how little they can explain.

My grandfather was a concrete thinker who had no time for fictions and fantasies. Questions like the insatiable Why were of no importance to him. Yet he had a kind heart, and instead of shouting, came up with a clever response:

"Why does the wind blow?"

"Because Why."

I remember hearing this for the first time and being completely stumped. He had answered the question too well. Why? Because Why! It was genius.

But I was a persistent child—some would say obnoxious. It took some thinking, but the next time his response came, I was ready.

"Why do we only see the stars at night?"

"Because Why."

My turn! "Why Because?"

I stumped him right back. I had won the battle, but the war was not over.

Eventually our conversations turned into a perpetual circle.

Why? Because Why. Why Because? Because Why. Why Because...

FOLLY OF THE WHYS

I found out much later that I was not the first to hear "Because Why." My mother and sister had heard that refrain many times in their own childhoods. And I began to wonder why myself: Why are children and philosophers constantly coming back to this question?

The problem with Why is that it is not used as a single question. The true Why has been buried beneath layers of confusion.

It has been mixed up with other questions, and the problem goes back at least as far as Aristotle in the fourth century BC.

In his works on *Physics* and *Metaphysics*, the famed Greek philosopher Aristotle asserted that there are four "causes" of a given thing: material cause, formal cause, efficient cause, and final cause. Material cause is the stuff something is made of, related to what we have called the What. Formal cause is the shape of something and its use, which is closely related to what we have called the Whence. Efficient cause is the What that creates a situation; the efficient cause of a cake is a baker. Though Aristotle's efficient cause does not exactly answer the question of the method process at work, it is implied, thus it is closely related to the How. Final cause is the purpose of a thing. The final cause of a chair is to keep the weight off your feet and your butt off the ground. For living things, especially people, the final cause is much more obscure.

For Aristotle, Why could be answered in any of these ways. Why has too many possible answers! Fortunately, our language has evolved clearer questions, as we have explored already. The "Five *W*s and an *H*" don't fit Aristotle's framework perfectly, but 2,500 years of change in culture and language will do that.

But this Why problem persists in its own way today. Today's English Why tends to have merely two types of answers, though both of those types of answers get a lot of attention.

The first type of answer to Why is actually a How. Why are there waves at the ocean? Perhaps it is better to ask: how are there waves at the ocean? Science may have a better answer than the alternative. How is the sky blue? What is the scientific process that lets blue light shine through, or what makes it appear blue in our mind?

The second type of answer to Why is related to the final cause, the purpose of something. This type of answer is far more complicated, and I strongly suspect that it is ultimately meaningless.

Why is a chair? What is its purpose?

I suggest that you take a quick moment to ponder this question.

The Cliffs of Why

...

How did that go for you? Now did you ponder the question, or did you try to think of an answer? Because that is the problem. Who determines the purpose of a chair: do you? Does the inventor of the chair? Does nature? Does some abstract notion of chair? Does a divine power?

The truth of final cause and the question of Why itself is that this is a question of power. Who authorizes, who decides what the purpose of something is? If the purpose of a chair is to hold your butt, are you violating nature if you stand on it to reach something on a high shelf? Are you accosting the natural order if you use it to stack a pile of books or laundry? If you sit on a tree stump, have you made it into a chair?

ANSWERING WHY

As the three-year-old or the college student repeatedly asks the "Why," a complex system of rabbit holes emerges, and the line of answering can wind its way down to unknown depths. It is a craggy and treacherous way down. Despite the many paths, there are only a few ultimate answers to the Why.

If you are patient enough to get to the end of the questioning, you will find that there are only two answers to Why: the Other and the Self. Consider the following:

Why does the sun rise?

Because the earth rotates around it.

Why?

Due to gravity and other cosmic forces between the celestial bodies.

Why?

It is worth reminding that the answers about rotation and physical forces answer How.

But arriving at this last Why, the final cause, the principle driving the action, there are several answers possible. "Because that's the way Nature works" or "because that's how God made it" are the two most common types of other answers. There are many variations amidst natural and supernatural others, and there can be follow-up Whys to be sure, but those end up in circles.

"Because I said so" is not helpful, but it happens. "Because I . . ." gets into the realm of human understanding and psychology. It too ends up in circles.

Why do you exercise?
Because I like to be healthy.
Why?
Because I like the way it makes me feel.
Why?
Because I want to be happy.
Why?

If somebody asks Why enough times, and the person asked has enough patience, the conversation will end up seeking unknowable answers. The Why will lead to the nature of the universe, which is unknowable, or the nature of an individual, which is also unknowable. Motivations are fickle, mutable, and impossible to verify. While the true Why may have no final answer, the way a person answers the Why can provide great insight.

WHY'S RULERS

How a person answers Why shows where they place authority. "Because I said so" means that the individual is claiming that their own authority is sufficient. "Because that is how the universe works" shows that fate is determined by natural forces. "Because God made it that way" speaks to the divine.

When answering the question of Why, you make a choice that reveals who you think is in charge of the matter. The true Why is the question of power.

These types of Whys can have some practical uses in philosophy or social sciences. They can reveal things about the way individuals and groups think, but asking Why on a cosmic scale merely reinforces personal biases.

The Cliffs of Why

Why can show purposes, intentions, causes. It can show all sorts of little stops along the way. Unfortunately, Why is mostly used as a vague, catchall question. It is often used as a question word when somebody does not have a question to ask. A child I once knew asked Why questions that were so vexing because they had no apparent answers built into them. Examples include "why is that a house?" and "why is that your nose?" Because . . . why.

It is time for us to move beyond this infinite digression.

No answer is truly best, but we need something that will get us past these cliffs.

Why? Who cares.

5

The Summit of Who

"Who are you?" said the Caterpillar.
This was not an encouraging opening for a conversation. Alice replied, rather shyly, "I—I hardly know, sir, just at present—at least I know who I was when I got up this morning, but I think I must have been changed several times since then."
– Lewis Carroll, *Alice's Adventures in Wonderland*

HERE WE ARE, TRAVELERS! We have finally arrived at the top of the mountain. We have reached the summit, the peak, the ultimate question. The question of Who—humble, noble, and magnificent—is the highest question that a person can ask or be asked. It is simple but far from easy. We can look back at what has led here: What we are is travelers; Whence we are is on this small stretch of life's road(s) together; How we are is by going through these questions; Why we are is . . . up to you!

The question of Who includes elements of all prior questions and brings them together in a way that leads towards ultimate meaning.

THE GREATEST OF ALL QUESTIONS

What is the Who? It is the ultimate question, the question that reveals the truth, the core, the essence, of a person. It shares features with each of the other essential questions, yet it builds upon their strengths and reveals a complete image of the person. It takes the What (type of thing), places it in a Whence (context), telling of many Hows (processes and methods), and considers the fluid Whys (little purposes) of an individual.

Who you are, Who anyone is, consists of changing states through places and times with different transformations and purposes.

You are the sum of your entire life—Who you have been, Who you are, and Who you will become.

You do not yet know Who you will be; and once your life is over, it is rather difficult to think of Who you were, because when your life is over you are dead. Yet while you will not know, your mark on the universe will be eternal and uniquely yours.

The answer to the Who is not a mere state but a story.

Who are you? You are the story of your life. And that story has a title: your name.

STORIED SPIRITS

Humans are not the only being with a Who. Animals have their own stories. They have changing purposes and states over time. Even amoebas, which are supposed to automatically respond to a stimulus with a mindless response, have different—albeit basic—motivations.

And creatures are not the only things with a Who. Consider the chair from the last chapter. Imagine the chair in your head. What type is it? A stool? A recliner? A toilet? A throne? A chair has its own story, though it is told differently from a human's. A chair's story comes from Who it has held and what has happened in and around it.

In my parents' spare room there is a steamer trunk that has, more than once, been a chair. The large chest of leather and wood held both the worldly possessions and the hindquarters of my great-great-great grandfather as he immigrated to the United States. At times it functioned as a coffee table. At other times it was a bench for the newest generation of youngsters. For a stretch of several decades, it stored old photo albums. These days, the steamer trunk holds up a television—an invention that did not even exist when that old, rugged chest was built.

That trunk has travelled across the Atlantic Ocean and the Appalachian Mountains. For about two centuries, it has supported the seats of grandparents and grandchildren—including relatives whose lives ended generations before my own had begun. It is the same steamer trunk—material fully intact—and it continues to have life as a chair, table, storage device, or TV stand. The steamer trunk has a story.

For a chair or a chest, it seems easy to say that it has been the same thing for generations, but is it so easy to say the same about a creature like the human? Are you the same person that held your name even a decade ago?

It is popularly said that the human completely replaces its cells every seven years. This statement isn't perfectly accurate—as some cells last much longer—but there is a truth at its core: our bodies largely change over time. Parts of our body break down and die and then are replenished with new materials that enter as food, drink, or breath. We are constantly replacing bits of ourselves on a cellular level. To go even smaller, our atoms are constantly changing, exchanging electrons, and combining or splitting to become something new.

Can we say that we are the same person from moment to moment, year to year, decade to decade? What is the continuity? What is the thread that holds our story together?

This is no new question. In the first century, Greek thinker Plutarch proposed a similar question about the "Ship of Theseus." Theseus was a demigod king and legendary founder of Athens who is also famous for slaying the Minotaur. His ship was preserved after his death, but as the wood rotted, it was replaced piece by piece. Eventually none of the original pieces remained, but it was still known as the Ship of Theseus. Was it still the Ship of Theseus? If not, at what point of renovation did it become something else?

You are a great vessel with your own name, and what holds you together through time is your spirit, your life. If that works for you, great! But if you find the previous statement a little too mystical, please take it up with me in Chapter One: What Things.

As living, conscious beings, it is easy to account for our continuity. As long as we are alive, the parts of us that are involved in that living system are a part of us. When you cut off your fingernail or lose a tooth, it is no longer a part of the present you. It was a part of your story for a time, but now it is in the past.

STORIED WORDS

The question of Who seeks to answer everything. It is magnificent and comprehensive. But therein lies the challenge. There is a problem with the Who, and it is not the question but the people considering it.

We simply cannot answer the Who completely. When we tell stories, when we listen to them or think about them, we select, emphasize, and diminish details. We leave out trivial points and forget morsels of truth. Furthermore, we embellish moments or emotions—sometimes intentionally but often naturally. Our brains only have so much capacity, and our mortal selves only have so much time. We cannot follow entire stories. We must truncate them with beginnings and ends, highlight the details we deem important, and move on.

While the great story of the universe might hold the ultimate answers to about any question we can think of, we mere mortals can only handle the gist of a few stories. And our gists differ based on our perspectives.

We take shortcuts. In an attempt to understand things bigger than us, we rely on the generalizations of the Cosmic Road. We use categories and types to fill in blank details of the story. We create familiar tropes and characterizations—stock figures like the wise, old magician and the reluctant hero. We create shortcut words that include ethical judgements: there is a noteworthy difference between someone being "bumped into" and someone being "assaulted," but both have been struck by another.

With shortcuts, we turn something complex into something simple. We speak of good and evil. Those who resist the forced binary of good and evil advocate for an ethical spectrum—a more colorful truth of reality. It is true that good and evil are too simple of designations, but not because of a sliding scale. It is because they are too vague—and generally unhelpful.

CHAIR EXAMPLE, NUMBER TWO

Let's take a moment for some potty talk. There is now a niche industry dedicated to bathroom books for children. We learn from a very young age that everyone poops. Pooping is as natural as breathing. For children, using the bathroom is a learning activity and a social event. For adults, pooping tends to become more of a personal endeavor.

The private pastime has its own style of chair called a toilet, potty, or commode. So how is it categorized when somebody's special stool is at the kitchen table? In the good-bad continuum, that would probably go toward the bad end. This answer is supported by a well-known adage to the effect of "one should not defecate where they take nourishment."

However, this stinky event could be shifted by mitigating circumstances. The kitchen pooper could be unwell or unable to control themselves. Is a baby morally good or bad because of where they don't do and where they do do? Despite the adage, pooping at a kitchen table is not inherently bad. Good and bad are not helpful ways of thinking about it.

Pooping at the table could be described as impolite, unsanitary, noxious, or accidental. Those words distill many ideas, but they do not over-distill into the good-evil paradigm. "Impolite" means that the action was not favorable for the social situation. "Unsanitary" has health implications. "Noxious" describes the sensory experience of the people around it. "Accidental" might describe the intention of the person who pooped. Rather than ascribing a supreme moral value, these terms tell part of a story.

SPECTRA

The world is not made of this-or-that, monochromatic binaries. The world is colorful, and we should take the energy to see the complexity of the colors, the hues and saturation.

Labelling things as "good" and "evil" is not helpful on the small scale. And on the large scale, the discrepancies between perspectives on good and evil only diverge further.

Good and evil might truly exist on an ultimate, existential scale. There may truly be opposing forces in the universe, a dualistic dual. The problem is: people have a bad history of agreeing on what fits as good or evil. Every individual in every culture sees this a little bit differently. Even the most ardent idealists within a cult will have fine differences between them. This is a fact.

Even if there is a distinction between true good and evil, nobody agrees on what it is. This becomes a problem when people categorize those who disagree with them as evil. This is a huge problem, and it happens all the time.

Good and evil are presented as ultimate, universal, eternal truths, yet no two mortals can agree on what things fall in those categories. What people actually mean when they use those categories is this: do good things; do not do bad things. That's it. That is the whole of ethics. Do good; do not do bad. Any words beyond those six either argue to define good and bad or imagine their causes and consequences.

So rather than good-evil or good-bad, it is more helpful to use terms with more complexity. Instead of saying smoking is bad, say that it is unhealthy. Instead of saying pizza is good, say that you find it tasty.

The Curse of Pharaoh

TRANSFORMING THE QUESTION

As promised since the beginning, this book was written to address the disquiet of life. Questions about pain, suffering, and evil have long histories. As long as we know, people have been pondering the good and bad things happening to good and bad people. These questions are known collectively as theodicy, which strives to explain apparent injustices in the universe.

Questions of theodicy start from two common forms: "why do bad things happen to good people?" and the inverse, "why do good things happen to bad people?" Taking the first form as the standard example, we can now apply what we have examined over the last few chapters and transform this unanswerable question into something a little more useful.

1. *"Why do bad things happen to good people?"* Let's first look at "bad things." Bad things are very difficult to determine. There are some things that are easily categorized as morally bad, such as rape, murder, and abuse. Despite the complexities of ethics, I think those are obviously bad. When people ask questions about "bad things," there is often a broader net being cast. Sometimes the "bad thing" is the death of a loved one or an accident. Is death bad? Does an accident carry a moral judgment? I have found that many "bad things" are often better described as "painful things." Is victory in war a bad thing? What about to the loser? I suggest that we change "bad things" to suffering. So instead, let's ask . . .

2. *"Why do good people suffer?"* Just as we are avoiding the value judgment of "bad things," let us also avoid "good people." Because of the spectrum of ethics, it is hasty to decide whether someone, even yourself, is good or bad. A person's actions can be examined in the context of their story, but this is a long, subjective process. Furthermore, when somebody is suffering, it is especially unhelpful to argue whether they are good or not. Instead, why not ask about all people? Every person has done at least one helpful thing and one harmful thing in their life. Let's look through the mirage at what this question

is really about: it is about you and people like you. This is true for me too. Instead of "good people," let's just acknowledge that this question is about "us." So instead, let's ask . . .

3. *"Why do we suffer?"* Yet if we stay with the Why, we are stuck looking for a personal motivation or a distant cause. The only possible answers are "because the universe simply works this way, or "because God/Allah/Krishna/The Great Spirit/Gaia/The Universe/Zeus/Cthulhu/The Force/The Flying Spaghetti Monster wants it that way." That can then lead down a further rabbit hole of Whys that has no attainable answer. Are divine powers motivated by malice, tough love, education, or something beyond our capacities? This is where the Why becomes opium, where the answers become more difficult to attain and less satisfying. There is no way to know for certain. Instead, let us ask the question in the form of a Who . . .

4. *"Who are we who suffer?"* Who are we? It is widely said that life is suffering, and we are alive. So to the original, slightly more specific question, "who are we who suffer?," we could further distill this to "who are we?," which is the core question of life itself, but that might be a bit too broad. Suffering is specific question about all of us. We all suffer in different ways with different causes, but we still experience suffering.

"Who are we who suffer?" asks a question about our relationship with experience, life, and the cosmic forces at play. We all suffer to varying degrees at different times, and there is no way to know how this experience will change as our lives progress. But one thing is certain: suffering is an inevitable part of life.

There are many external forces that can cause us suffering, forces beyond our control. What we can control is how we respond to those things outside of our power. External responses reveal our internal selves and shape our stories.

The Curse of Pharaoh

VIRTUE AND VILLAINY

Virtues and vices, while poised as ethical opposites, have a twin meaning. Both are "actions repeated by a person over time." Virtues are actions declared good; vices are deemed evil.

This book is about a villain. We did not take this path together to merely stamp the titular Pharaoh as evil or vice-ridden. Instead, it is important to call him a villain.

Where calling something evil is an ethical statement, a villain is a character in a story. Villain is a storied word that describes someone or something who has aims different enough from your own that they come into active conflict. A villain is an opponent, an adversary, one who stands against the "hero."

When you encounter a story, establishing the hero is one of the first things you do. You latch onto a character. You root for that character. That character is your hero. (If you root for a hero that does some ethically "bad" things, you might call them an anti-hero, but this is a new term for the same idea.)

You are the hero of your own story. A villain is anyone or anything who stands against you. It can be a rival, an illness, an unnamed force, a task, or a goal. The villain is the role of your opponent. A villain is an adversary, one who stands against the hero. You can be your own villain too, and maybe there are times that you stand divided—in favor and opposed to yourself. You can be hero and villain at the same time.

The great Saint Mr. Fred Rogers famously blessed the children with refrains of "I like you just the way you are." This affirmation is admirable, and his accepting and welcoming nature is one that we should strive to imitate. It is good to like and love the things that are pleasant rather than things that are not. But when taken to its extreme, this can lead people to stagnation.

If you find that you are getting in your own way—that you are also the villain in your story—then you have made a profound step. It is the beginning of an epic and ongoing personal journey.

The Summit of Who

We constantly change, for better and worse. We grow and decay, consume and produce. Change is as inevitable as suffering, and they often go together.

Here at the summit of this question of Who, we will take a brief rest.

Then, when you are ready to proceed, the true exploration will begin—the exploration within. We will abide and meditate upon the story of that great villain, Pharaoh. And in it, perhaps we may find some insights into our question: *who are we who suffer?*

PART II: *Character and Villainy*

6

If Only

A REAL TRADITION

Spoiler alert and adult content warning: this section should be previewed before being read by anyone under the age of 13.

ONE OF MY FAVORITE childhood toys was an old cassette player and recorder and a pile of hand-me-down tapes to play on it. I had the story of *Peter and the Wolf* as narrated by Sir Patrick Stewart, some Beach Boys and other oldies, and other miscellany that my family didn't mind a four-year-old messing around with.

Among these treasures was *The Night Before Christmas*. It was narrated by Wilford Brimley and came with a pop-up book to follow along. I loved the story, the rhyme, and the fact that I could pretend to read along. Maybe even more, I took in the pictures—the careful detail, the dimension, the contrasting colors. It brought my imagination to life.

But up in my mind there arose such a clatter, I couldn't articulate what was the matter. Until when I asked my parents at last: tell me the truth, and tell me it fast!

They had a plan.

My mom and dad had prepared for the day that I came asking about the big man in red. They had carefully crafted a line that gave scientific truth without ruining the magic.

"Is he real?" I asked.

"He's a real tradition." They responded. It was practiced, ready, a silver bullet of rhetoric ready to take down any vampire that might ruin my childhood.

I admire their effort, but I didn't take the bait. I repeated the question, and they repeated the line. Finally, I said, "So he's not real." They gave up the ghost.

I was young, and this was a hot topic among my friends. I told my best friend—not to ruin it, but so he too might know the truth. He told his parents, who insisted that Santa was real. He took their side.

To this day I'm fascinated by this "real tradition." Partially for the history and partially for the psychology.

Saint Nicholas was a real guy. I've written elsewhere about him, about how during his life he voyaged around the Mediterranean, punched a heretic, and provided dowries or gold for poor girls who would have otherwise become enslaved, trafficked, or homeless. Because of this, he is the patron saint of sailors, pawn shops, and prostitutes (among other things). We celebrate his generosity to this day, though globally his legend has morphed and diverged into many visions of the magical gift-giver.

Tall tales of Saint Nicholas are particularly strange. As in the case of my friend, parents and adults share these legends with children, knowing that they have long since diverged from the truth. When asked why, the general response is "for the magic."

Despite his real roots in tradition, the Santa in department stores is fiction.

USEFUL FICTIONS

The If is the conjunction of truth. It is a curious little word. It is simple, but it is the hinge on which so many questions rely. Its answers are not always clear: "if something is" and "if something is not" do not appear to be the only options. Fictions and lies both present untruths, yet they are quite different. Truth itself is a whole other matter. "If" is also a gateway to alternate and potential realities. When wielded humbly, it can have great benefits; when wielded with greed, it leads to pain.

Fictions demonstrate this strange relationship with the truth. Theatre, literature, film, and games are just the beginning of the realms where people find fiction. Mostly we know that these are not true. At the same time, the best fictions are those in which the partaker not only consumes, but becomes consumed. In 1938, Orson Welles presented *War of the Worlds* on the radio. The Halloween broadcast of the forty-year-old story famously led some to believe that an alien invasion was occurring. The breadth of panic is likely exaggerated.

In 2003, Random House published Dan Brown's second novel, *The Da Vinci Code*. Despite its location in the fiction aisle and the fact that none of its creators claimed it to be true, clergy and historians alike are still answering questions from earnest believers who are convinced that it is true.

Fiction is a tool that can clarify or mirage the truth. Fables and parables—like those of Aesop, the Brothers Grimm, and Jesus of Nazareth—are tools to teach the lessons about the truth. Though racing turtles and talking frogs are generally not considered real, these stories show something about reality.

On the other hand, this tool can hide the real. Fiction can provide an entertaining escape from reality—a break from the harsh world or a healing catharsis where you can feel and do things that cannot really take place.

When fiction is treated as fiction, it can support healthy individuals and societies. When this tool is wielded incorrectly, when it is disguised as truth, it becomes a weapon. The hammer that built now destroys.

When someone effectively uses lies to manipulate others, they are tarnishing this fantastic tool. Not only this, but their flagrant defiance of the truth reveals something else: fear.

A lie demonstrates fear of the truth. The truth can be harsh, but denying it does not change it. The poor coward who relies on lies must first deceive themselves into believing that they can sculpt reality for others. They must then wield their malicious spirit to force that truth on others. Yet reality abides, waiting to reveal itself. Anyone who imagines such a power over reality shows that they are not only a coward but also a fool.

UNREAL PROBLEMS

During the criminal trial of Jesus, Provincial Governor Pontius Pilate asked, "What is truth?"

The relationship between people and reality is a strange one. As we explored with the Whence, context and perspective influence the way we perceive whatever is really going on. We experience reality through our senses, which are interpreted by our brain. These are imperfect hunks of meat and electricity, but these are the tools we have, the beings we are. When we share our experiences with each other, we can get a better idea of what reality is. Each of us sees through a tainted, twisted, and scratched lens, but if we share what we see, we can get a little closer to a picture of what is.

Our picture of reality is an old puzzle left in a basement flood. There may be pieces missing and damaged. The guide photo on the box is faded. Each of us has our own little piece, and we do our best to put them together in a way that makes sense. Sometimes we almost get it right. It will never be perfect or complete, but the closer we get, the more grounded we will be.

With a grasp on what *is*, we can consider what *was* and what *could be*. The If allows us to imagine what then comes. If we mix red and blue, then we will have purple. If we do not, we might mix the blue with yellow and then have green! We can imagine more possibilities, outcomes, or solutions—and we do! We predict what will happen with weather, behavior, horse races, online purchases, and baby due dates.

With the If, we can envision utopias and shining lives! "If I wake up early and run, I will feel better inside and out!" "If we all got along and agreed to stop being greedy, we could save the planet and humanity!" The If can lead to exciting futures. It can help us imagine what can be and can help us find the steps to make dreams reality. It might seem hokey or naïve, but it is true. The If allows us to form ideologies—hopes for and ways to achieve and idea or the ideal. Ideas are not real because they have not (yet) been actualized. Despite not being real, ideas constantly affect reality.

The If also has a downside.

If can lead to fearful futures. "If we do not stop this together, we will go extinct!" This can be paralyzing or motivating, but the If of the future is not the most dangerous.

The most dangerous If for an individual is the If of the past. The If of the past leads you into the whirlwind of the three Harpies of Regret: Shoulda, Woulda, and Coulda. These three consume you from the inside out. "If I had known I *woulda* known. I *coulda* done something. I knew I *shoulda*, but I didn't."

I know those who are constantly haunted by these. Regret swirls in their minds as they imagine what the present reality could be, but is not, and cannot be. Woulda, Should, and Coulda are all children of the If of the past. "If only I had said something." "If only I would have chosen the other." Maybe you Coulda, Woulda, and Shoulda.

But you didn't. I'm sorry.

ANOTHER W: THE WHETHER

As for us, we will not linger too long on these questions of If. If is another *W* in disguise. If you read the heading above, you will know that it is Whether. Whether or not something is true, real, or factual is usually important for navigating daily life.

As we prepare to dive into the realm of Pharaoh and his story, the If, the Whether, provides an opportunity to make an essential point about this journey we're taking together: the historical factuality of this story is not on the docket.

The Whethers of this story are not at stake. Whether you believe that this story is a historical reality, an embellished legend with kernels of truth, or a fanciful work of fiction, we will make use of the story for its own sake. Pharaoh has a real story, a real lesson, and most of all, a real character.

This story is an archetype, one that has incarnations everywhere. More importantly, it is one that we can learn from. Whether you believe this as a factual historical account or as the fable of an ancient tribal religion, this story is one of the few "real traditions" that has become important regardless of its factuality.

For this exploration, it is not the history under examination, but the story. This story has been told for generations—over three thousand years! As history, we can learn from the examples and mistakes of those before us. As a fable, it can serve as a lesson from our ancestors to us today. Whether fiction, fable, or historical recounting, this story can teach us something true from ages past.

7

Pharaoh Pharaoh

WHAT WAS HE?

HE WAS A PERSON, a human. He had human body, a human mind, a human spirit, a human life. His journey began as yours, mine, and every other human's: in his mother's womb. He was a particular arrangement of meat and electricity that had some resemblance to you and me.

WHENCE WAS HE?

His womb was not the same as yours and mine. He grew in the protective womb of ancient Egyptian royalty. His mother was the bearer of the divine emissary, the top military officer, ruler of the land; he was the chief custodian of divine, civil, and military order.

He was born naked and frail, a helpless mortal, capable of nothing but pooping, suckling, and crying. Yet his was a royal cry, one met with every luxury and amenity available. Even his diapers were the garbs of a king.

His tutelage was unmatched—the wisdom of old, the practical teachings of war and governance. All needs were provided through tutors, bodyguards, servants, chefs, generals, viziers, wives, concubines . . . Free from the cares of commoners, Pharaoh was able to focus on higher things.

Every movement was hallowed. Was it the power of the gods subduing the world so to seat him above it? Perhaps it was a social contract—the collective will of his society to be ruled and protected by him. Perhaps he was nobody special, an accident of history, mere happenstance. Whatever he was, the context of his birth meant that he would be treated like one with great power.

HOW DID IT HAPPEN?

Everything was gilded. From his birth, his ascent was known by everyone he encountered. By acknowledging his status, they reinforced that reality. His influence grew; his spirit reached across the land.

After this Pharaoh had grown, years into his reign, a long-lost prince named Moses returned to the land as a sage. Rather than reclaim his proper position of power in the court, this sage stood before Pharaoh's throne as an outsider. The sage claimed the local enslaved population as his people and asked to take them into the wilderness to worship a foreign god.

Preposterous! Pharaoh was the living link to the divine, the mediator of celestial affairs. It was *his* role to bridge the human and divine. And this former prince, this imposter, this sage dared to stand before the greatest king and highest priest! He dared to claim that his people should celebrate their own foreign festival apart from Pharaoh's great civilization! He dared to take them away from their work—Pharaoh's glory—for days to worship some strange and other divinity! How dare he even consider asking!

Furthermore, this sage could not even speak for himself. Moses stood in Pharaoh's court with Aaron. Together they delivered the message: Moses as the mystic, Aaron as the mouthpiece. They performed miracles in the name of a divinity that Pharaoh did not know. Outrageous!

Pharaoh was not impressed. His own sorcerers could do the same simple tricks—turning a staff into a snake, defiling and cleansing skin with leprosy. This is basic magic. Such signs could not persuade Pharaoh that Moses and Aaron wielded any power that could threaten his own. Pharaoh remained unmoved.

Until it began.

The nation's water turned to blood. Pharaoh's sorcerers supposedly could do the same, though this time they could not reverse Moses' and Aaron's magic. The Egyptians had to dig deep to find fresh water. It was the first plague, the first strike against Pharaoh.

Frogs came next. Once again, Pharaoh's sorcerers claimed that they could perform the same trick. Despite this, Pharaoh asked Moses and Aaron to pray the frogs away in exchange for allowing their festival. When the frogs died away, they were shoveled into stinking piles. Pharaoh did not keep his end of the deal.

Pharaoh's sorcerers had reached their limits. When the gnats came, they were so swarmed that they said it was "the finger of God"—the condemning power of a divinity that they could not control.

Moses approached Pharaoh at sunrise warning that future plagues will only affect Pharaoh's kingdom, not the enslaved people. When the flies came, Pharaoh once again asked for prayer in return for letting the people go into the wilderness. Once again, when the problem was gone, so was Pharaoh's promise.

Then the livestock. He may have taken notice that the enslaved still had their animals while those of Egypt fell dead.

Then boils, which covered even the sorcerers.

Again, Moses met Pharaoh at sunrise to warn him. Six plagues had struck Pharaoh and his people. Was the point not clear? There was a divine power that was unknown and unsatisfied by Pharaoh. With all that had happened, could Pharaoh not see that he could have been crushed like it was nothing?

When the storm came, Pharaoh trembled. Hail and lightning struck terror into his people and destroyed their flax and barley crops. Pharaoh summoned Moses, pled his guilt, and promised for a third time to let the people hold their festival in the wilderness. For a third time, his promise vanished alongside the plague.

After the storm, Pharaoh's officials counseled him to let Moses, Aaron, and their people do what they please—let them appease this God of plague! Pharaoh eventually conceded, asking Moses who is required to attend this wilderness festival. When Moses answered that every enslaved person would be leaving, Pharaoh rejected the extreme request. How dare this Moses! Who does he think he is!

When the locusts came and destroyed the remaining crops—the wheat, spelt, and fruits—Pharaoh begged for forgiveness. The locusts were carried away on the wind, and to nobody's surprise, Pharaoh refused to let the enslaved people go and worship their plague-making deity.

Darkness struck with no warning. Unless, of course, you count the eight plagues that had already occurred. Pharaoh relented once again, saying that the enslaved people could go and have their festival. Moses and Aaron reminded Pharaoh of something that should be a given to a mediator of the gods: proper ritual required sacrifice. That meant that the enslaved people needed to take their livestock too.

But that kind of sacrifice would mean that there is another divine power—one that Pharaoh does not control. Those slaves dare even imagine that they have some divine connection above Pharaoh! Did that sage Moses think that he could truly wield a power mightier than the great Pharaoh? He would allow no such nonsense. Pharaoh told Moses and Aaron that if they make any more such requests, he will show them power; he will take their lives.

Moses and Aaron departed from Pharaoh's throne but not before making a cryptic threat: the firstborn of Egypt will die, and Pharaoh's officials will bend before Moses. It is a wonder that Pharaoh let them leave at all.

In the dark of night, death found the firstborn of Egypt.

Pharaoh was devastated.

In his fury, he summoned Moses and Aaron to his throne for the last time. Though their death would have been more satisfying, his rage and sorrow were tempered by fear. He sent them, their people, and their livestock away immediately. In his desperation, he did not forget to ask to be included in their prayers.

And so Moses and his people fled in haste. In the wilderness they worshipped. They ate humble bread and gave thanks for their children. They carried the bones of their ancestors in hopes of claiming their homeland. As they moved through the desert, they took care to avoid settlements and conflict.

Reports of Moses and his people winding through the wilderness reached Pharaoh. His painful losses from the plagues only fueled more rage. Why would anyone want to live under anyone but his excellence? What ungrateful wretches! Their lives as slave under his benevolent hand would seem blessed compared to freedom under anyone else!

HOW DID HE TAKE IT?

Pharaoh had lost so much already. His dream of power had been dismantled before his eyes. With the blood-water and frogs, his absolute domination over a fertile utopia was the first illusion to go.

Then the gnats and flies, the death of livestock, and the plague of boils outclassed his magicians, who saw that their power was nothing. Pharaoh began to waver, but his doubts were overruled by his resolve.

The great storm and locusts destroyed the crops of his land. He would not be able to provide for the people he ruled. He was failing as divine emissary, unable to keep cosmic balance.

His absolute control, confidence in those around him, his ability to create prosperity—these were being stripped away from this man of power. But these were an appetizer platter preparing him for the main course.

Darkness struck—a prelude for the shadow of death that came next. When the firstborn of his people fell dead, Pharaoh had been cut off from his power over time. His legacy, his people, his rightful heir—they were dead. He caught a glimpse of his own mortality.

Despite this, he held on to his delusion of supremacy. Losing his control, confidence, prosperity, and legacy were not enough to redirect one so corrupted by power. He had failed to maintain cosmic order as the high priest. He had failed to manage a prosperous land as king. Other people wanted to worship something other than him, and he took it personally. He refused to yield that anything or anyone—human or cosmic—could have power above his own. He only wanted to maintain his imagined control.

HOW DID IT END?

So he exercised his one remaining role of power. With everything else gone, he only had physical force. He led his chariots, his army, to reclaim the people that escaped his generous rule. As the military's high commander, he accompanied the sword of his civilization with his own blade in hand.

As he chased his prey, he was hindered by fog and fire. His resolve did not relent. These were merely a nuisance, a distraction from his real mission. The muddy ground under the chariots would not stop him either.

Until it did.

The peasants he chased seemed to have no trouble crossing the riverbed on their feet. Pharaoh's chariot wheels stuck in the mud. The soldiers grew panicked as they grew still in congealing mud. They shouted that a greater power was fighting them. The pursued had cleared the riverbed while the pursuers stood armor-laden before the unstoppable tide.

WHY?

Because why.

WHO WAS PHARAOH?

What is the character of his spirit? How does his story end? What is the role that makes him a villain? Can he be redeemed?

Could we say that he needs no redeeming—that he is a hero? After all, this pharaoh is a model for ones who "do what you believe, no matter what other people think!" Is he a martyr? A saint? He is persistent, value-oriented, and tenacious! He fights for his rights! He fights for his freedom! He defies cosmic forces for this freedom! Should we not admire this freedom fighter?

But that freedom he fights for is for him and him alone. Pharaoh is so self-centered that everyone else is his opponent. He is a villain through and through.

Though the final moment of his life is not described in this story, there are three plausible endings. The first, and least dramatic, is that he was so focused on reorienting his troops and his mission that he did not notice the water until it was too late. This is not only unlikely but terribly unsatisfying. After everything we have heard of Pharaoh in this story, a mere accident of unexpected death just doesn't fit.

More satisfying is the second, more poetic ending. Perhaps in the instant before he died, Pharaoh had true clarity. There is something satisfying about the romantic moment of a repentant villain. Not only do they get theirs, but they know why they deserve it. Perhaps Pharaoh felt remorse at his own past cruelty. If would be even more satisfying and redeeming to his character if he were struck with genuine humility. Overwhelmed by the wall of sea, he might have realized his own smallness, his true place in the universe. He would accept such a death as justice, a consequence of his own arrogance.

But I have seen villains up close, and their endings are not so lovely. If Pharaoh is truly the villain, then the ending without regrets is the most realistic ending. Rather than submit to the greater power, Pharaoh damned himself by his own hard heart. Instead, he stood like a fool, cemented in the mud of his pride, cursing whatever power plagued him.

A true villain, Pharaoh saw that the universe was in error and he stood right. He believed in his own perfection—and that some flawed power was issuing him injustice. He had been stripped of his earthly power, but the illusion remained. As the walls of water crashed down, he looked up toward the heavens and cursed whatever or whoever was looking back. The curse came from Pharaoh himself.

A VILLAIN'S FATE

On the shores of his watery grave, the freed people sang with joy. They played the tambourine. They danced.

8

The Mighty

THE MOST OFFENSIVE OBJECT IN THE WORLD

ACCORDING TO MY RESEARCH, the most offensive item in the world is the bacon cheeseburger. The broadest reason for its potential to offend is religious doctrine. Followers of Islam, Hinduism, Buddhism, Judaism, and Jainism currently account for over 2.5 billion people—a third of the world's population. Each of these religions have guidelines prohibiting or limiting the consumption of pig, cow, or meat altogether. While religious sects and individual followers vary on exactly what doctrines they adhere to, these dietary guidelines are still widely regarded among those religions.

But religion is not the only reason that this item causes tension. It is estimated that there are just shy of four hundred million vegetarians in the world. Vegetarians and vegans have diverse reasons for their dietary habits, including personal health and preserving planetary resources. A trope of these believers is that they freely share their dietary preference and reasoning without being asked. Despite being the butt of such jokes, their conviction is admirable. Some vegetarians are probably also counted among the religious observers, though I know of no estimates of how many more people that might include.

The Curse of Pharaoh

Beyond vegetarians and adherents to some major religions, there are socioeconomic forces that add to the infamy of this calorie-laden sandwich. Bacon cheeseburgers have become associated with the hedonism of Western imperialism and globalization. They are expensive, and there are many in the world who cannot afford the indulgent sandwich. We should also include some of the people who have enjoyed too many of these sandwiches and have since been instructed by their doctors to stop eating them, or else.

I know of no other dish—or any object at all—with so many prohibitions, objections, and negative associations.

None of these restrictions currently apply to me. Though I try to be respectful of other people and their beliefs, I do occasionally enjoy a bacon cheeseburger.

Some of the people who eat them, however, I take issue with.

More than a few times, I've seen people treat other people like garbage over this item.

Here's the typical scenario: somebody requests one, pays for it, waits. When the burger arrives, something is wrong. It wasn't cooked long enough. It was cooked too long. It has the wrong toppings. It's supposed to have another slab of meat on top. The bun has sesame seeds on it.

Sometimes when you order food, it doesn't arrive as expected. It is extremely rare that this happens on purpose. Yet I hear these customers berate and belittle the very ones who are trying to serve them this luxury.

It is a shame. Such behavior is a stain on civilization.

People object to orders and treat people rudely over every food possible. What is so special about bacon cheeseburgers?

These simple masterpieces display some of the crowning achievements of humanity. The bread, lettuce, and tomato can be mass-produced thanks to the ancient advent of agriculture. The beef, pork, and cheese are available thanks to skillfully domesticated livestock with safety practices that limit the breakout of disease. Cheese, bread, and ketchup come from sophisticated cooking techniques and traditions. The vegetables and wheat are harvested at different times of the year, but thanks to refrigeration and growing capabilities, these are available year-round. Because of transportation efficiency, the parts of this modern marvel can come together so that a bacon cheeseburger can be assembled virtually anywhere on earth, in any climate, at any time of year. And thanks to cooking techniques, careful kitchen logistics, and communication technology, a bacon cheeseburger can materialize from a whim in mere moments.

Each one is a monument to human achievement.

But hold the pickles, please.

The hands around a bacon cheeseburger wield power. This is such a power as Pharaoh.

But here, my fellow traveler, is a harder truth. Skills and resources are also forms of power. The very ability to read this, the time you are taking to consume these words, the time I have taken to write them—these activities are the exercise of our power.

THE TRUTH ABOUT PHARAOH

I am Pharaoh. You are Pharaoh. We are pharaohs.

But we need not share his fate. We need not share his curse.

Before we can learn lessons from Pharaoh, we must accept the truth that we are pharaohs. If you do not feel ready to accept this as a truth, then I ask you to at least entertain it. The lessons from Pharaoh are for you and me, because in us is the potential to become like him (if we are not already). The lessons we learn from Pharaoh are not so that we can point at other people and feel superior, proud of our own enlightenment and smugly tut-tutting at all those other fools. That is what Pharaoh would do.

In order to stop being a pharaoh, you must acknowledge that you are a pharaoh. That is why this comes before the first lesson. From this starting point you can learn. You can avoid his mistakes. Know that you hold power—a gift that came from elsewhere, a gift with limits. Use it wisely.

PHARAOH'S GIFTS

From here we begin to learn from Pharaoh. He had been given everything. He had been built up, standing above a nation, unaware and uncaring that his pyramid of power was built on the labor of other humans, not some divine blessing that he especially deserved.

Power made him a pharaoh. His path toward villainy began with how he responded to that power. To borrow a term from Chapter One, a Tyrant specter led Pharaoh to force his spirit and power on everyone he encountered. He took it all for granted, just as the cruel customers ignore the great energies of human progress and sacrifice that have brought the bacon cheeseburgers into their hands.

Hubris, entitlement, arrogance: these are some of the names of the poison that turns the powerful into the wicked, handing them over to the specter of the Tyrant.

From arrogance grows selfishness—a fearful lust that hungers for its own life. Pharaoh positions himself to receive—be it power, praise, or precious resources. He collects these like a dragon who only exercises his energies in pursuit of more.

Pharaoh clings to great power but claims no responsibility. The biblical book of Luke, in its twelfth chapter, explains that great power brings great responsibility. This popular proverb (paraphrased by Spider-Man's uncle, Ben Parker) is not a direct reflection on Pharaoh, though it would have served him.

A villain takes false credit for their own good and falsely blames others for their own faults.

A villain claims that any inconvenience or perceived slight they experience is a great injustice that has befallen an innocent saint.

For the powerful to avoid this is simple, though not easy. Attempting to understand and appreciate the power that you have is a good first step. You are a pharaoh. We are pharaohs. We stand like pigeons on the shoulders of the fossilized behemoths that made our civilization possible.

Pharaoh failed to realize what he was. Though he was powerful, he was human. He was the inheritor of the trust and legacy of a culture that held his position and his person as their sovereign ruler. But he was still human.

The wicked pharaohs of today reenact his failure. They call themselves things like "self-made." They claim, and seem to believe, that they picked themselves up by their own bootstraps, ignoring the reality that not everyone even has boots. A famous musician will say, "nobody believed in me" after millions supported them by listening to their songs, going to their shows, and buying their merch.

TEACHING YOURSELF

When I was a child, another child told me that she taught herself to read. At first, I was amazed, but that quickly wore off. I realized that it was impossible. A person can catch on if they have a knack for something, but they cannot teach themselves to read. That would require them to understand the complex symbol system of the alphabet without anyone telling them even what they are. That would require their mind to spontaneously create the same symbol system with no external input. It's nonsense. It relies upon generations of people creating written language and tools to learn it. It takes countless people to teach anyone to read. Since then, I've heard the phrase many times. With the possible exception of the inventor(s) of language, nobody has ever taught themselves to read. We all have the help of people, tools made by people, or both.

Instead, know your power. Acknowledge that it is a gift you did not earn. This is the first lesson of Pharaoh, and it has immediate benefits. When you realize that your power did not come from you, you can see that it is not yours. When you understand the sources of your power, you can realize their extent; you can look down and see the giants upon whom you sit.

Life depends on so much. Pharaoh had it backwards. He thought that the lives of so many relied on him, not realizing that he relied on so many. Existence itself is only possible because of what has existed before. The power we wield did not originate with ourselves. We are inheritors of power.

THE RAVAGED

The sad reality is that the power of Pharaoh was taken from others. The great structures that were built during his reign were done by the calloused hands and bruised bodies of others. The land that he ruled was claimed and captured through conquest. Pharaoh and his ancestor exercised their wills to plunder from others.

Just a few lines before this, I wrote that "we are inheritors of power." Every person is the heir of an oppressor, and there's a good chance that every person is an heir of a victim. You may not have taken the villainous steps to conquer another, but we all reap some benefits from these conquests.

The biggest pharaohs of today leave crumbs for the many—just enough to keep us alive but so little that we fight over their scraps. Like dogs under the table, we fight and beg while those big pharaohs above us feast. At the same time, some of us manage to hoard scraps taken from others—becoming little versions of the big pharaohs. The little pharaohs look down on those weaker than them for fear that they will lose their little hoards.

Little pharaohs could look upward at the bigger pharaohs who have enough to feed everyone. Instead, they often become satisfied with their stash. They become lieutenants of the big pharaohs by protecting their bits of comfort from the ravaged, instead of fighting to get more for all to share.

A little pharaoh will use their little power against those with even less. The bigger pharaohs do not truly care for their little lieutenants. They see others only for their usefulness—as servants or subjects, not as people. And like the Pharaoh of our story, they do not care who they drag into the mud.

LITTLE PHARAOH CRUMBS

I have been trying to avoid editorializing or making all this Pharaoh business just about me, but here I must interject. I write this as an employed White male living in the United States—all of which are categories that signal inherited power. I also belong to marginalized groups, but I will refrain from spelling those out. I fear sharing them—not because of rejection by the powerful but because I do not want to overshadow the marginalized and ravaged people who do not wield the power that I do.

I am not always sure that keeping quiet about belonging to those groups is the right choice.

But I interject for this reason: there are so many powers that are given in the culture around me that come from others being ravaged. This land's native population was devastated by disease, with those who remained being killed or removed. The industrial revolution that brought the world into the modern age was built by the muscle of enslaved peoples, desperate immigrants, and laboring children. Medical science and procedures that are now commonplace are the results of monstrous experiments by psychopaths and grifters. Most clothing and consumer goods are cheap (or at least affordable) because they are made by people who are being exploited on the other side of the planet. Almost every inch of the land on this planet is soaked with the blood of someone who once occupied it.

Some say that the victors write the histories, but that is not wholly true; it is the survivors who write the history. Some survivors try to give voice to the dead; some relive their own traumas and recount their own horrors, so that others may learn from ink and paper what they learned in blood and screams; some are powerful manipulators who rewrite past and present to make themselves the hero. I do not recount these things here to ruminate on our guilt. (I have done that elsewhere.) I recount these things merely to recognize that we have power because of others.

POTENTIAL PARALYSIS

Recognizing one's own power and privilege can be an overwhelming shock. Those with little power, especially the ravaged, are stripped of many potential choices in life. Those with power are in constant situations with boundless choices. Many retail chain stores in the United States—grocery stores, drug stores, department stores—have an entire aisle dedicated to toothpastes. Most of the toothpastes have the same two or three active ingredients; most of them have a similar selection of flavors; most of them are within the same price range. How do you pick?

Thinking about this quickly becomes overwhelming. Do you get the cheapest? There might be dozens at the exact same lowest price point. Do you get the one whose flavor reminds you of childhood? Do you get the one that claims to have the most ethical sourcing? Do you get the one that guarantees the most opulent white smile? Do you find a local craft toothpaste company that harvests their own fluoride from aged tea leaves? Do you try to figure out what toothpaste defines you as a person?

Power and privilege bring countless toothpaste scenarios, especially regarding what and how you consume. What food you should grow? What should you buy premade? What should you order in bulk? What type of vehicle might you need to get around? What style of home—and where? More power means more possible choices. More possible choices mean more possible consequences. More power, more choice, more responsibility.

If you have capacity for empathy and become aware of your power, it can become paralyzing. You might fear the consequences of your every action because of the harm it might cause. It is good to avoid harmful action! But the world is complicated, and you cannot fix everything all at once. Even if you are powerful, you are not the ultimate power yourself. Breathe deep, fellow traveler, and prepare for the first lesson of Pharaoh.

THE FIRST LESSON: PACE YOURSELF.

Yes, you have power. Yes, you have responsibility. But you are still mortal. You are not a god who has the power to control reality with your whims. Pharaoh tried to wield his power for his own ambitions, but he became so entrenched, so stuck in his ways, that he thought he could do anything. He could not. You cannot. You have great power but not unlimited power.

Pace yourself. Distance runners will tell you to "run your own race." This applies to 5k races, marathons, and your mortal journey. Live your own life.

Pace yourself.

As a younger man, I felt like I needed to find a great, noble purpose or cause and that I had to have selected my life's ambition as an adolescent. I had friends who knew they wanted to be engineers. They were going to take CAD (computer-aided drafting), physics, and calculus. Then they would go to college for engineering. Then they would become engineers. I thought I had to have a similar focus for my life path. I had a difficult time choosing what life path to follow. Do I work toward a job that will save the world? Do I find work that will give me lots of money, which I can then use to save the world? What does the world need? What matches my skills? What will there be a market for? How did those engineering people nail it down so early? Maybe there's just something strange about engineers.

It took me well into adulthood to realize something: life is not always short; sometimes it's long. That was terrifying. When life is long, paths that seemed apparent can divert, twist, or disappear in a landslide. Careers, families, physical abilities, interests, economies, resources, skills, friends, environments, and beliefs change. You run the distinct risk of being around for a while and experiencing some big changes. It's a long life. You have to pace yourself.

When I began teaching at the college level, I encountered "nontraditional students," sometimes called "nontrads," who were older than me. At that point I had some professional experience, and was close to earning a PhD. My older students had just started working toward their bachelor's degrees. Sometimes they would express a confidence that came from their life experiences. Sometimes they would express shame or embarrassment for being in classes with students half their age.

These nontrads brought worldly perspectives and a certain level of discipline to their work. They did not take their education for granted. They chose to be there. They did not go to college just to go to college; they went because it was the next step toward their chosen goal.

It is only half of a joke when I say that I needed extra school because I did not get enough the first time. I have, many times, thought about what life would have been like if I pursued other things instead of going straight to college after high school. I first went to college because I thought I was supposed to go to college; those nontrads went to college because they had discerned what they wanted to do and what skills they needed to do it. I am no better a person because of any particular accomplishment, and neither are they.

We have to run our own races. You have to live at your own pace.

PHARAOH'S FIRST FOLLY

Julius Caesar, at 33 years old, was climbing through the power structures of the late Roman Republic. Legend holds it that he was reading about Alexander the Great, who had created one of the largest empires in history and died at the age of 32. Thinking about his own achievements next to Alexander's, Caesar wept.

Julius Caesar lived to be 55 years old and became the first ruler of an empire that lasted—depending who you ask—for over one thousand years. For two thousand years, his name (and variations such as Kaiser, Czar, Tsar) were attached to the rulers of empires. And only a century ago, they named a salad after him! (OK, the salad was named after the chef Caesar Cardini, but guess where Caesar Cardini's first name came from.)

Historians can fight each other about who was greater. Yet neither Alexander the Great nor Julius Caesar had ever, in their life, earned a driver's license, ordered something online, or even learned to recite the United States Pledge of Allegiance at the start of their school day, things which are commonplace for children in my culture. It is possible, however unlikely, that they could have eaten a bacon cheeseburger.

Comparing your own accomplishments to someone else is a painful game. It is a trap that so many like Pharaoh fall into. They have so much and become obsessed to clinging onto their power. They become solely concerned with having more and being better. Empires invade and expand. Billionaires seek more riches. Celebrities crave more attention, so they sell their souls or morph their bodies with scalpels and injections. A pharaoh runs everyone's race but their own.

IMAGINING POWER

We sometimes imagine what it would be like to be a bigger pharaoh. I regularly hear people pondering what they would do if they suddenly came into great power or wealth. Sometimes their wishes are quite selfless, quite responsible.

"If I could be rich like them, I would solve world hunger, homelessness, and fix the environment!"

"If I had that kind of money, I would donate most of it to charity."

"If I were a billionaire, I would be Batman! I would fight evil and help my city."

There is only one problem: the people who say that type of thing do not understand the character of a person who can hoard that sort of wealth or power. One does not gain extreme wealth and power because of their generosity, empathy, or care for the world. Humility and other selfless values are exchanged for such power and wealth.

Some foolish pharaohs say, "Whoever dies with the most toys wins!" What they win has yet to be seen. As far as I can tell, they end up like everyone else. Sometimes the box is fancier; I'll give them that.

At best, it seems, some of the world's richest will leave their remaining wealth to a charity or a foundation. To say it another way: they give up their wealth over their dead bodies; wealth and power must be pried from their cold, dead fingers. The closest thing to a true act of kindness is either a tax break or just leftovers.

If any extremely wealthy or powerful person ever reads this (and acknowledges that they are extremely wealthy and powerful), I dare you to prove me wrong. Be generous! Give it away! Your gifts should help others!

For the rest of you, the same idea applies: do not trade your humanity to become a bigger pharaoh. Do not fall into the trap of such cravings. They only leads to deeper holes of desire, jealousy, and greed. You do not need to imagine being anybody but yourself. You are enough.

So for now, take a breathe deep. Pace yourself. When you are ready, move on.

9

Diligent Blips

LONG AGO I HAD a friend named Froggy. He was gifted, mind and body, with special skills in grammar, vocabulary, history, and distance running. He was a pharaoh like the rest of us. When college placement exams approached, he told everybody how well he expected to do: maybe not the very best in the class but close. He bragged all the way until test time, which was going to be his time to shine. This test score would be the sign that we should revere his amazing knowledge. He took every opportunity to boast about how easy they would be.

Test time came and went. Results came back. He did well. Nothing amazing but nothing to be ashamed of. He would be able to get into a decent college without any trouble. But after his score came back, he was not the same—his rhetoric changed. Suddenly, those standardized tests were not a good measure of your knowledge or intelligence. He would say, "These tests only tell you how well you can take a test."

He boasted his skill, invented a competition, and then lost. He was ashamed.

ON COMPETITION

I felt for Froggy. I have overdosed on the brew of competition. The external motivation that we can get by comparing ourselves to others is a stimulant for sure. Such stimulants can make us stronger, smarter, better, but they must be used with great care and greater moderation.

Being the best is not merely standing over others. Competition is external, superficial. It makes an activity about something else. It narrows your vision, taking a single external measure and wagering everything on it. If you want to be the best because of a single test, you will not be satisfied. Even if you succeed, you will not be satisfied.

In any realm of competition, loving to play and loving to win are very different things. If you love to play something, you will pursue it, improve your skill, and find joy whether you win or lose. If you love winning, you will go outside the boundaries of the game to win. You will cheat and your victory will be hollow. Players love to play; cheaters love to win.

There is much talk today about being your best self, living your best life. If every facet of your life is measured by how others live, you will be chasing an imaginary hybrid of their perceived success. Though it is not real, I have seen this beast. It has a head that reaches to the heights of interesting hobbies and culture. It is sleek, fit, and stylish. It is strong enough to do it all, yet it walks on carefree feet. It is a bizarre monster, a questing beast that you will never catch. It only exists in the realm of imagination.

You have great power, but it has its limits. Though we have power like Pharaoh, we must avoid the illusion of supernatural superiority. Remembering true human nature—a unity of body, mind, and spirit—we recall our hungers, fervors, and our need for rest. Human power has limits, and when we ignore these limits too often our potential cannot flourish.

FOR WHAT IS POWER?

Sadly, it is easy to find examples of those who are given much and do so little with it. Imagine a refrigerator full of the best fresh ingredients. They could be cut and cooked into culinary delights, delicious foods, amazing concoctions. Or they could be wasted, and the refrigerator would become a cold chest of rot. There are many fridges full of rot out there.

But what kind of thing should you be using your ingredients for? What is a fitting use for your great power? You have so much potential. How can you know what is right to do with it?

The answer is simple. That is, it is in simple things—boring, ordinary, mundane things. Those with the most power do not merely stand on top of the mountainous heights of civilization. They must also learn to climb.

For the powerful to remain unspoiled, people must learn chores. The basic maintenance of life—cleaning, laundry, dishes—these are the beginning of properly using power. Though they may seem unconnected, that is just the dread of chores tainting your view. Chores are not always pleasant, but they are always necessary. Somebody has to do them.

Even more, chores are endless. My friend Mae is a dynamo in the science of chores. Her tireless energy creates a space where others can thrive, though she knows that the perfectly clean can never be. There is always another dirty dish, stinky shirt, garden weed, dusty trinket, floor fuzzy, or fleck of dirt. The war of chores can never be won, but it can be lost; the battles are worth fighting.

A major inspiration for this book is *The Myth of Sisyphus* by Albert Camus. Camus reflects on the story of the wicked King Sisyphus as a model for the human condition. The tyrant was condemned to spend eternity pushing a rock up a hill. For all eternity the rock would fall as he neared the top. Then he would have to start all over again. Camus proposed that when the rock fell, Sisyphus smiled. Despite the eternally meaningless activity, at least he had something to do. It is like an itsy-bitsy spider gladly climbing a waterspout after being washed out by the rain.

Successful chores do not require Camus's perspective. Chores are not meant to distract you from your existential fears, though they can. Instead, they channel your energies into something positive, constructive, and human.

Tending to your basic needs is to attend to your basic humanity. Every person needs hygiene, tidiness, and organization.

By these things we create. We take disorder and turn it to order. We make new things, inspiring and beautiful. By performing the mundane, we make space for extraordinary things.

Chores are practice for creating order, which paves the way for you to create. Your energies are in motion, moving, structuring. These are the component parts of creativity. Instead of merely consuming, you can use your power to make something new.

To create is to emulate the creator. Whether you believe that the universe came from impersonal forces, a personal deity, or something(s) in between, there was some creative force behind it. By creating, we allow the energy of that creator to flow through us and perpetuate the creative process at work in the cosmos.

We can channel the cosmic energies within but not perfectly so. Our creative process shares our mortal limits. In order to create, we must destroy. For a chair to become, a tree must die. Yet if we do not create, disorder and decay will do their work uninterrupted. Creation, like chores, can never be complete, but it is worthwhile.

COMPASSIONATE CONVENTIONS

Alongside chores, there is another mundane, boring, tedious activity that will help us avoid Pharaoh's rotten superiority: manners. Manners are sometimes for your benefit and always for the benefit of the other.

Manners are not always simple. They are signs for mutual well-being, but they are not always welcome ones. If you are genuinely trying to attend to the person and the context, then you are doing right. On the other hand, politeness in excess can be more harmful than rudeness itself. This is clear in traffic. When one person yields when they should go, they hold up the cars behind them. Their over-politeness benefits one improperly at the cost of others and can cause confusion, accidents, and more traffic.

Manners are conventional. They are predictable and expected in their home context. Not only do the words themselves benefit others but the action of doing them. The actions should not be hollow, but sometimes they will feel that way. When we learn manners as children, they are extra bits, buffering quirks, forced prompts of "what do you say . . ." But somewhere along the way these little add-ons start to mean something and make good citizens.

Manners are handy signs, to you and from you, of genuine care. They can give a quick impression of you and your values. But they are not universal signs. If another does not share them, then they were either taught a different set of manners or perhaps were not taught any at all. In some cultures, it is polite to ask a person how they are doing; in others, such a question is intrusive. There are many books about different manners and gestures in different cultures around the world.

Despite the difference in form, all manners have a common goal: they connect people. They help connect people in several common ways across cultures. Manners tend to fall into the categories of (1) wishing well-being, (2) seeking favor, or (3) thanksgiving.

Wishing Well-Being

Wishing well-being means wanting good for another person. A greeting or salutation at the very least acknowledges the humanity of another person and at best explicitly wishes them well. Some cultures find it innocuous to ask you "how are you doing?" because it is implied that they hope you are well. Other cultures find the question invasive and prefer to keep personal affairs private. That does not mean they do not wish you well.

A farewell literally means that you want someone to be well. "Goodbye" comes from the phrase "God be with you," a literal blessing with many equivalents, such as the Spanish *vaya con dios* ("go with God!"). Some languages share a common word for greeting and farewell, all of which wish for some sense of peace or wellbeing: *aloha* in Hawaiian, *shalom* in Hebrew, *salaam* in Arabic (which sounds similar and is related), *ciao* in Italian, and *chao* in

Vietnamese (which sounds similar but is unrelated) are just a few examples. Acts of generosity are well-wishes in action.

Seeking Favor

Seeking favor is a time-related category of manners. To seek favor before an action is permission. To seek favor after an action is an apology. Either of these is a request that can be granted or denied by someone who might be harmed or inconvenienced by the action. Contrary to the popular saying, it is almost always better to seek permission first rather than forgiveness later.

Thanksgiving

Thanksgiving or gratitude is the same no matter when it is used. Thank you (in advance)! Thank you (for what you are doing)! Thank you (for what you did)!

Just as chores prepare you to create, manners prepare you to connect.

But you might not always feel like creating or connecting. They are good activities, but we need rest too. We certainly do, and rest has a role in our creativity and connectivity. Rest allows for recovery. Some cannot create at all unless properly rested. This also applies to connectivity. Resting from connections allows us to recuperate, re-center, and reflect upon who we are. With this self-awareness, we can connect to each other and the universe by acting more authentically.

And who are we who create and connect? What is our aim, and how does that form us? Should we create just to say that we are creating or connect just to say that we are connected? Doing these activities just for the sake of doing them is miserable. Even more miserable is doing the basic activities for no apparent reason. (Cheers, Sisyphus!) Chores and manners with no clear purpose are vain, confusing, and just don't feel good.

A SPECIAL NOTE ON APOLOGY

Apology means acknowledging a higher sense of values, a power that takes priority over your own indulgences—whatever they might be. It also means acknowledging the importance of the person or people to whom you apologize.

A true apology describes the action, accepts the blame for doing the action, and makes a promise to correct the damage and/or not do that action again. A false apology speaks to the reaction of the victim, not the pain they suffered. "I am sorry I hurt you" (a good apology) is very different from "I am sorry that you got upset." A person who cannot, or does not, apologize shares the selfishness of the villainous Pharaoh. Here I must apologize for my own strong feelings, because I can think of nothing kind to say of people who will not apologize. I find the refusal to apologize disgusting. I hope I can do better.

Those who learn to apologize well also learn to take comfort in the healing of others. Beware of over-apologizing as well. If you apologize for things that are not within your control, you are pretending that they are within your control. "I am sorry that the weather is bad" is not an apology, because you cannot control the weather. (At least I assume not.) But it does present a challenging quirk of the English language. I am not aware of a conventional way to say "I empathize with your feelings about the unfortunate weather" that does not make it sound like you have the power to do something about it. Perhaps "I feel bad about the weather too" is an acceptable substitute. In any case, proper apologies are an important part (but not the only part) of learning to find some of your own happiness when another person thrives.

THE SECOND LESSON: GIVE A HOOT!

Using our creative energies and becoming connected only feel significant when we feel them leading somewhere. So to make these activities worthwhile, find something to care about. If you care about something—whether it be a cause, a person, or a power—your activity starts to have purpose and meaning.

A family friend and financial analyst, Jim Cassidy, was brought up in the Catholic school system and has stuck with the religion all of his life. He remembers the nuns at his school telling him not to waste paper. Jim is approaching retirement now but still uses the smallest Post-it notes he can find and writes as small as possible. Those nuns still influence him—even though they are long gone. A few bits of paper doesn't seem like much, but it is still something. It is a principle that they taught him that has stuck.

Do what you can to make things better. But also, remember that you cannot fix everything. The world is a very big place, so start with what is around you before you try to fix the whole world. One problem links to another, like the mythical hydra with its many heads, and they eventually become overwhelming.

Remember the first lesson: pace yourself! Facing the hydra of cosmic problems can be just as paralyzing as getting caught in the void of meaninglessness. Start working close to you—what we called the Personal Road and Local Road, places where you have direct connections—before becoming consumed with cosmic roads that are beyond your reach. (Sometimes the Personal Road and Local Road are not geographically local. If you have friends or family around the world, then your Local Road is not all in the same physical place.) You rarely have to look long or far to find problems that meet your passions.

Purpose is where problems meet passions. Pharaohs fail to notice any problem that is not causing them direct discomfort. On the other hand, being a good person does not mean that you have to solve every problem out there. You cannot give all of the hoots. Start by giving one.

PHARAOH'S SECOND FOLLY

Pharaoh had no care outside of himself—no external to direct his energies and connect to. He was self-absorbed and self-important. To make matters worse, he had servants to attend to his chores and did not have to use manners because all manners were built around respecting him.

The pharaohs of today face the same problem. They do not know what it means to attend to the basics. They have no concept of respecting another for the sake of that person. Chores are beneath them, and other people only exist to serve and further empower these powerful demagogues. Their creativity is destruction; their connectivity is damaging. And they don't give any hoots.

Pharaohs even take this a step further. Pharaohs see other people as either useful (in that they can be manipulated) or suspicious (in that they are trying to take something). To a pharaoh, generosity, compassion, and vulnerability are weaknesses. They eventually come to believe that everybody else is like them. Because of that, they lose the ability to trust. They lose the ability to love. In the game of power, there are no teams. How horrible that existence must be!

But we can learn from Pharaoh's mistake and avoid his fate. Find something to care about, something that allows you to be generous, compassionate, and vulnerable. If you're not sure where to start, just pick the next thing that comes along! (And if it doesn't turn out after a while, try something else!) There will be something soon. Find it, and give a hoot!

10

Crash and Foam

RAINY DAYS

As a ministry intern, I was visiting a group of preschoolers to chat about any churchy things they wanted to know more about. I tried my best to speak on their level, and they were good sports by following along. When it was time to leave, a few of them had final thoughts to share with the group. "My favorite food is brownies." "My mom works on taxes." "I like bunnies!"

One little girl with a raised hand candidly stated, "It's raining." The straightforward melancholy in her voice hit me deep. My response of, "I'm sorry" was genuine, though I knew I had no power to change the weather. But she didn't linger in this sorrow. She stared up with resolve: "Rain makes the flowers grow."

I don't mean to overblow a trivial interaction, but why stop now? That was fourteen years ago, and it has stuck with me. It was the drama of her transformation from sorrow to strength. I assumed that she was consumed with sadness, but I underestimated her. She didn't merely look on the bright side; she knew the whole picture. She showed me the big picture with that simple wisdom children know so well.

Difficult days are a fact of life. Some days start off rotten; others merely finish that way. Some days bring simple misery; others drag you into existential despair. I don't know if any other creatures are aware of their status as mortal flecks, but no other animal that I know of spends as much time ruminating on it as us humans.

Though we will probably manage to get wiped out of existence much sooner, the sun is set to consume our planet in about seven or eight billion years. At what point will every trace of us be washed from the universe? Will our atoms have even the slightest effect on the trajectory of an exploding star? Will our entire species make any difference in the long run?

We might share the fate of most good ideas: you, me, our species and this book may be lost, forgotten, inconsequential. But this murky pool of depressing reality is not the whole picture.

The pit of meaninglessness and angst takes me back to my adolescence. Good times! But even those teenage years—awkward and painful as they can be—are also not the whole picture of life. Most make it through those years into awkward adulthood. All adults got there from childhood.

The deep void of futility is entrancing—its emptiness captivating. Meditating on the vast nothingness can help put things to scale. Life's fortunes and misfortunes can be viewed humbly.

An ancient king sought wisdom to keep him sober in times of joy, and hopeful in times of trial. "This too shall pass" replied a sage. And they since have passed—the times and the people. All pain comes to an end; the same is true for joy.

But the void speaks, providing both perspective and a great deception: It is so great that it can appear to be the ultimate meaning of everything and the true big picture. It is not.

When stuck staring into the void, the answer is simple: look somewhere else.

AVOIDING THE VOID

Another famous adage hits this from another side: "you don't know what you have until it's gone." And it is well-established that everything will be gone. But knowing that things will not exist someday does not mean you have to despair.

The Curse of Pharaoh

There are two main ways to deal with the void. One way is demonstrated by my dear friend Cammie. Growing up is hard. As we entered adulthood, just hanging out whenever turned into getting together. And getting together turned into occasions. Time grew between trips, and we ended up spending more time catching up and reminiscing than making new memories. We all knew what was happening, but Cammie was especially sensitive to this natural growing apart. When we would gather, Cammie would spend the whole time missing everybody—mourning that we would all be parting again soon. Rather than enjoying the fact that we were there, Cammie, to the visible annoyance of some, spent the whole time focusing on our absence in the future. There was so much good to see all around, but she was staring into the void.

We still gather occasionally; Cammie still mourns. She is not wrong that we will not always be together; it's just a bummer.

The other way of dealing with the void is a common theme in self-help, mindfulness, martial arts, yoga, and Jediism. Be in the moment. Enjoy the now. This happy approach is not a license to be reckless and ignore the future. It's the freedom to embrace what is. It is stopping and smelling the roses. It is realizing that the bright side is part of the picture; the void is only part of it.

Focusing on the joys of now gives you the ability to appreciate what you have when you have it. You can love what-is, not just what-was or what-will-be. Because what-is is not what-was, and what-will-be might be nice too.

This is finding the Whence in which you live—the when, the where, the here, the now.

Cammie's premature nostalgia skips the moment. She values it so much but is driven by the fear of its loss. Her mind is stuck in a Whence that is elsewhere and elsewhen. The Harpies of Regret—Shoulda, Coulda, and Woulda—haunt her past and infect her present. We still love her.

Crash and Foam

THE LONG CRASH

Pharaoh had the opposite problem. He took his pleasures, his privileges, his joys and comforts as givens that would last all of his days. He took for granted all of his powers. He ignored the present because his future had always been guaranteed. He did not know about the void until it was too late.

Piece by piece he lost everything. Piece by piece we can see that nothing belonged to him in the first place. The river of blood, the frogs, the gnats, and the flies showed his lack of power over nature. The livestock growing ill, the boils, hail, and locusts destroyed the human technologies of agriculture. The darkness and death showed the weakness of mortality. Pharaoh had lost all that he thought he had power over. He could not subdue nature. He was not in control of his society's well-being. He could not control the forces of the cosmos.

As these layers peeled away, his resolve softened and hardened again and again. When he gave chase to the fleeing slaves, he wielded the last power he held: the sword. He still had coercive force over his army and anyone they encountered. But even his army was made useless by a simple vulnerability—they got stuck in the mud. Finally, he pursued with all that he had left—his own chariot, his own sword, his own life. And as the waves crashed down he lost the last of his powers, his life itself.

Such is the fate of every power of every person.

There is a nobleman named Jacques in Shakespeare's play *As You Like It* who personifies the specter we called the Cypher in Chapter One—the one that overdevelops the mind at the expense of the body and spirit. Jacques's mind was so dominant that his body trembled and his spirit shook with every breeze of change. He waxed on the perpetual sorrows of life, concluding that even if one makes it through life, the final trial will take everything. He said that long life would bring "second childishness and mere oblivion, sans teeth, sans eyes, sans taste, sans everything."[1]

---

1. William Shakespeare, *As You Like It*, ed. Francis X. Connor (Oxford: Oxford University Press, 2024), 5.7.65-66.

Pharaoh lost everything not because he was wicked but because he was mortal.

I knew a man called High Pockets. High Pockets lived through the Great Depression and worked hard at whatever job he had. His parents saved up to buy him a drum set, and at fourteen he started playing weekends with a band. He then trained then as a mortician, a funeral director. After his car was hit by a drunk driver, he could no longer lift bodies to do the job. He opened a candy store—which back in the day also sold Coca-Cola, Camel cigarettes, and locally churned ice cream. The neighborhood families knew him and liked him.

Time passed, and the children grew up and moved out of the neighborhood. Years of drumming took his hearing early. Age slowly took his teeth and eyesight. He lost his sense of taste after a bad fall. He lived a long life—so long that he outlived nearly everyone he knew. The mortician who couldn't lift, the drummer who couldn't hear, the candy man who couldn't taste, the friend with nobody around. All who knew High Pockets said he was a saint. But alas he went—sans teeth, sans eyes, sans taste, sans everything.

There is an old adage that is sometimes attributed to Scots or Norwegians, which says, "It could be worse, but don't get your hopes up."

THE PERFECT REUBEN

The fate of Pharaoh and High Pockets can strike us in the short term as well. An unfortunate colleague of mine, Marshall, took me out to lunch at a good sandwich shop. As we mused over the menu, the Reuben sandwich caught his eye and sparked his memory. Marshall began to recite a well-rehearsed monologue about how once, long ago, in a deli in Florida, he had eaten world's best Reuben.

I'm no connoisseur of the Reuben sandwich, but Marshall's description was mouthwatering. The corned beef was thick and juicy, the marbled rye bread perfect in texture and toasting, the sauerkraut mild, the Swiss cheese was rich and nutty, the Thousand

Island dressing had not over-soaked the bread. I cannot do justice to the poetry in his words, his voice, and his eyes. In the final verse of his eloquent prose, he lamented that he would never have such a perfect Reuben again.

He then ordered a Reuben, which he was ultimately unable to enjoy. I ordered a bacon cheeseburger, which was pretty good. I pitied him.

THE VIRTUE OF VEGGIES

There are so many variations on dealing with the void, each of which carries its own set of risks. Cammie's premature mourning embraces the inevitable but misses present joy. Pharaoh ignored the future and was not prepared to deal with the pain it brought. High Pockets lived a good life but couldn't avoid fate. Marshall was poisoned by memory.

There is a place in between—a place that the little girl found when it was raining. There is a place where we can acknowledge the reality of mortality and still find the joy of the moment. There must be a way to remember what was good, savor the moment, and hope for the future that still bears the reality that one day the things that are will not be.

Learning to see the whole picture is a challenge that takes practice. The virtue of vegetables shows how this happens. Children are notorious for resisting the greener variety of produce. Frustrated parents often see piles of veggies left on the plate long after the other elements of dinner are gone. That pile of green bitterness becomes an obstacle between the child and the sweet desserts of their desire. After a while I found this sequence happening in my own eating experience. I would enjoy my mac and cheese and meatloaf, but then that stinking pile of little trees would hold me up. Like children throughout history, I tried to leave the table, claiming that I was full before my parents could hold me to task. But alas! I was required to finish at least a portion of my veggies before leaving the table.

This was the pattern until one day I realized another way. I had been starting with the tastiest bites, then I was left with a bit more misery in each bite. Rather than the slide into displeasure that inevitably crashed into a wall of veggies, I flipped the curve. Instead, I turned every meal into a crescendo of joy. I started with my veggies first, then gradually moved toward the better foods. Each bite tasted a bit better than the last, so that the last bite I ate was the tastiest.

It's been a long time since this childhood discovery, and my approach has not changed much. I survey each food to decide which is best, then away I go! But in these decades, something has changed. I grew accustomed to veggies from eating them first—so much so that I now enjoy the broccoli that once haunted the corners of my dinner plate.

This is the virtue of vegetables: when you make a habit of eating the vegetables first, not only is the rest better, but the vegetables themselves begin to taste better. The difficult, tedious, bitter parts of life—the chores, the paperwork, the routine—can become more tolerable when they are not left to wait.

I have another method of getting gratification out of mundane and miserable activities. It is an attitude that has developed from helping somebody worse off than me. I take on these tasks for someone who is weaker, more forgetful, lazier, dumber, and needier than I am; I get the work done to help Future Me. I wish I had discovered earlier in life how unreliable Future Me really is. If I leave the dishes in the sink, that lazy bum will not do them either. If I leave my clothes in the dryer, Future Me will dewrinkle them a half a dozen times before he gets to them. Future Me detests paying the bills if he even remembers. So I try to think of Future Me. I pity him and try to help him out as much as I can, because I think he will appreciate it.

Incidentally, Present Me often appreciates when Past Me has done my grunt work so that I can relax a bit.

THE THIRD LESSON: ENJOYING OUR MISERY

I was sitting with a couple once, helping them prepare not only for their wedding but for marriage. Among the advice that dribbled from my mouth was something that struck the bride-to-be so much that I now make sure to tell it to all hopeful couples: enjoy the misery. Married life is regular life but with another person who you trust to support you through all of the highs and lows. Every person experiences sickness, health, plenty, want, joy, and sorrow. Enjoying the misery for marriage means realizing that somebody said they'll stay with you through it and that you can care for somebody enough to stick with them through it too.

But for an individual, single, married, or whatever, you can learn to see the good times and the bad as a part of a picture of your whole life.

UNDOING THEIR MISERY

Now is a fitting time to remind you that this is written for those with power, those who wish to be generous and not wicked as Pharaoh. We cannot ignore the people enslaved by wicked pharaohs. Wicked pharaohs commit inhuman atrocities, becoming crushers of spirits and monsters who steal lives. Wicked pharaohs manipulate, abuse, and oppress. The reason to bring them up now is because the misery they cause is not normal or natural.

To counteract the wicked pharaohs, we must use the powers we have to help the suffering regain the power, safety, and life that properly belong to them. Telling someone who is truly suffering—who is being dominated or tortured by a wicked pharaoh—to enjoy their misery, or that their pain is part of a bigger picture, only adds to their suffering. That is not the misery I was talking about enjoying.

Cruelty creates complications for those who wish to live a peaceful life. It is not good to wish harm upon others, but where is justice when wicked pharaohs go unpunished? It is difficult to enjoy any moment when you become aware that others are being enslaved elsewhere. How can we have complete joy until suffering has ended, until lives are properly restored.

While learning to enjoy the miseries of daily life, we cannot forget to give a hoot.

PHARAOH'S THIRD FOLLY

When we consider Pharaoh's downfall, we see a difference between those with power and those without. Those who have nothing to lose have insight as to what is important. Those who have much are corrupted by what they think they own and are poisoned by the fear of losing it.

Pharaohs end up in a most pitiable position. They get caught in a cycle of craving. They live only to satisfy those cravings. And their attempts can never live up to their expectations—either not being satisfying enough or not satisfying for long. They eventually lose their very ability to enjoy anything at all.

The Pharaoh of our story was in a unique position to gain insight. He had everything slowly taken away to the point where he could look his own mortality in the face. He lost so much but still had his life. When the illusions of power and ownership were taken away, he could have looked up into the sky and had the clarity to see his proper and tiny place in the universe. Going from having everything to nothing in such a short time, he could have gotten a good view of the whole picture. He could have seen the good of what he held for such a short time. He could have appreciated the luxuries of his brief life and looked toward the sky with gratitude. Instead, like so many, he imagined that his temporary luxuries were permanent and that what was his to use was his to keep.

The wicked Pharaoh looked up to the sky and cursed the power that had blessed him in the first place.

Pharaoh was rich in possessions, richer in folly. Surrounded by fortune, he suffered.

You can find blessings in this moment, the one you're in right now, give a hoot about others, and enjoy your misery.

Either way, the crash will come.

11

Life in the Wake

A PERSON CLAIMING KNOWLEDGE that they cannot explain has no knowledge at all.

Wisdom, information, and ideas are all connected to other wisdom, information, and ideas. There is no secret island of knowledge that is separated by a vast sea. Knowledge is always close to other knowledge, even if it is sometimes more difficult to reach.

Knowledge from the olden days has been preserved and passed to us. While technology has advanced our knowledge in realms such as health and agriculture, the wisdom of the past still has something to offer—especially in reflection on the human condition as a whole.

Sages and survivors of old have recorded their knowledge, but old scrolls are not the only well of ancient wisdom. Poems, stories, and songs are laden with hidden meaning and rich insight. Looking at this ancient story of Pharaoh is no different. Before considering the final lesson, we will recap the first three.

A SUMMARY (IN CASE YOU FORGOT OR SKIPPED THE REST OF THE BOOK)

You have some of the powers of Pharaoh, but you do not have to be like him. Our power does not come from ourselves. Pharaohs think that power belongs to them. This is the beginning of their pain.

Recognizing your own power allows you to use it well. You can begin to understand where it came from, how much or how little it can do, and most importantly, that power is not something to hoard for yourself but to use for others. For this you must pace yourself—running your own race, living your life and nobody else's.

Competition is about defeating others, not improving yourself. Disciplines of self-care, attending to basic chores, and using manners keep you grounded as a human being. A pharaoh does not allow themselves to do such simple things as apologize, and they become untethered from real human relationships. Find a cause or a person and invest yourself. A pharaoh only sees others as useful or threatening and slowly loses the capacities for trust and love. By investing yourself with others, you can grow, love, and see the love that is given to you.

Sometimes life sucks; it can and will be hard. Suffering is pain without understanding. Pain is guaranteed; understanding is not. Live in your Whence; see the gifts around you, and remember that the pains and joys will all pass. We will lose everything; that is just how it is. Your power, your life, your comforts, your capacities will all go away. It is OK. It is not because you are good or bad; that is just life. So learn to enjoy the misery of life, and make it less miserable for others. Do not just seek to satisfy your own cravings, but seek the joy in things as they happen.

THE FINAL LESSON: SHAM ON

You have no say in how reality works and surprisingly little say in how the real world changes around you. But you do have some say in how you experience reality. It can be a slow, difficult process to transform the way you experience reality. It takes energy, attention, and intention, but it can be done.

If we take the pharaoh powers we have and use them for good, we can become simple sages. A simple sage does not star in stories.

Life in the Wake

A simple sage is not a Stoic philosopher, an enlightened Buddha, or a holy saint. They are just a simple sage, and that is plenty.

Life is full of muddy conflicts, few of which can be resolved. The problem of ethics—living the good life—has no shortage of voices who are ready to tell you what you should do. If you disagree with one opinion, you can easily find advice telling you to do something else. But reality is more complicated than fabricated little ethical scenarios. Good advice is hard to find and harder to apply.

Life happens in real-time. Many choices do not come with time to think or consider the best options, if there even are best options. When you consider your principles, a seemingly simple problem can turn into a complex whirlwind. Do our mundane choices—soup or salad, which toothpaste to use, what shirt to wear—have a best answer? A simple decision can lead into a rat's nest of ethical dilemmas.

But when it comes down to it, you have to choose your answer. And yes, even doing nothing is a choice.

Here lies the final lesson of Pharaoh: sham on.

A sham is confident, if not correct. Sometimes you have to pretend, to fake-it-till-you-make-it. Do the best you can and get going!

Get moving. Ever forward. Keep on rolling. Boldly go.

When you pace yourself, give a hoot, and try to enjoy the misery, you're still going to mess up. Those messes are important and will help you avoid the trappings of the wicked Pharaoh.

But when you mess up, getting trapped ruminating on every past mistake, worrying about the slightest error, will paralyze you. Allowing the best to become the enemy of the better will only make you worse.

Keep going and you will get somewhere. Learn and experience new things. Explore.

You do not need to lose your foundation or forget your origins to go out and explore. You can "know where you came from" and still "be where you are."

Pharaoh was stuck in one position in one small sliver of the world. He had no idea how small he was or the great potential of what he could have been beyond his little world. Exploring and moving on does not mean that you have to travel (though you certainly can). You can read new books, talk to new people, walk a new way, make something new.

Try something. Mess up. Try again. New experiences will lead you to new ways of thinking, new ways of being. You will become a new character.

This feels a bit like a pep rally and a motivational poster but it's real. Push forward. You can slow down, pause, rest, and stop, but don't get stuck.

This might sound simple, but for many people it is exceedingly difficult. To keep moving, growing, and changing, you have to understand that reality does not rely on your perfection. This is a mindset that you can develop by pacing yourself, giving a hoot, and enjoying the misery.

You will make mistakes—not because you aim to but because we are all limited. We are not gods with cosmic powers. We are people who are just trying to be decent.

Do not let fear of messing up keep you from doing good things. Go after it. Do not get caught up in defending your missteps. Learn from your mistakes. Try again.

Sham on.

THE SONG OF THE SIMPLE SAGE

And there we have it. The lessons of Pharaoh: pace yourself; give a hoot; enjoy the misery; sham on. By knowing your power, caring about someone or something, finding contentment in the whole picture, and venturing onward, we can avoid the trappings of that wicked Pharaoh long ago. We can find joy, not just satisfaction. We can love and trust others, not just use them or fear them. We can find purpose in making life better for others and find happiness in simple joys. We can take solace in our decline, still seeing small gifts and blessings along the way.

Life in the Wake

Perhaps we can rephrase these lessons into a single metaphor, a poem that will help us stay afloat in the floods of life. Pacing yourself, controlling what you can, is like moving your own body or rowing your own boat, no matter how big or small. Giving a hoot means that you choose to be compassionate and gentle as you move through the paths of life. Enjoying the misery is choosing to find joy, appreciation, and merriment in your travel. And that final lesson—sham on—is where you can choose to experience the world in a happy or hopeful way. Our mind interprets reality, does it not? We create visions, imaginations, dreams of how it all works. When you put this together, you find that there is some other old wisdom at play—wisdom that you learned a long time ago.

> Row, row, row your boat;
> Gently down the stream;
> Merrily, merrily, merrily, merrily;
> Life is but a dream.

Around we sing, and on we go.

Life and happiness don't have to be complicated, do they? Thanks for travelling here, for sharing this time with me. Go well, my friend. Go well.

Epilogue: Birth and Rebirth

So, I suppose I am a pharaoh.

The girlfriend from the "Preface: In Retrospect" section became my wife, and we celebrated with a once-in-a-lifetime (probably) trip to Jamaica for our honeymoon. To accompany my lounge chair by the crystal waters, I took a stack of books to last the week. Like Pharaoh, I was privileged; unlike Pharaoh I was not content to marinate in luxury. However, I did make sure the reading was fun. It was a combination of graphic novels and philosophy books.

The graphic novels were awesome, several of which came from Marvel's Noir universe. The philosophy books included Soren Kierkegaard's *Fear and Trembling*, and Camus' *Myth of Sisyphus* (which I covered briefly in Chapter 9: "Diligent Blips.") I had no idea beforehand that these books were connected.

Fear and Trembling introduces the idea of the "leap of faith," that has since become a popular phrase. It is the final step toward becoming a "knight of faith," who has found true happiness. Kierkegaard based this idea on the patriarch Abraham, who was commanded by God to sacrifice his firstborn son. Abraham's "leap of faith" was when he raised the dagger to strike his son. As the knife plunged down, a divine messenger stopped him, and Abraham was rewarded for placing his faith in the ultimate power.

Camus' *Myth of Sisyphus* is built on the story of a despotic king who was condemned by the gods of ancient Greece to push a boulder up a hill for all eternity. As he would approach the summit, the boulder would fall, and he would have to start again. Camus argued that Sisyphus smiled as that boulder rolled down, because it gave him something to do. Against Kierkegaard, he argued that life itself was as pointless as Sisyphus' punishment, and we should find contentment by staying busy during this meaningless life.

(A note to my dear philosopher friends who might object to these summaries, please go easy on me. These are not essays on existentialism and I am, at best, a novice philosopher. Because why.)

I was inspired by these books and spent a lot of time in Jamaica pondering what story, tale, or legend might be the next step for these—this Abrahamic story (retold in several major religious traditions) and this Greek myth. I wanted to respond to them, but didn't know how. Should it be a superhero story (many of which I hold dearly)? Who would be my prototype? What would be the Ur-story, the core legend?

More than just a story, what moment in that story is the point that makes it matter?

I did not solve that question during my stay on that beautiful island.

As we packed up to fly back to the States, an early summer storm dumped on Puerto Rico to our east, causing a cascade of travel delays throughout the Caribbean. Being late to leave Jamaica, our flight also ran late to arrive for our connection in Atlanta.

Like years before in that Philadelphia bus station, we had to spend the night in a transportation hub to await further transit.

Some might call it bad luck. We were stranded in the Atlanta airport with no immediate way home.

Then again, we were relatively safe. We had climate-controlled shelter. We had access to food and whatever amenities were available in the airport vending machines. (The shops were all closed.) We had each other, and a deck of cards.

I heard loud gripes from fellow travelers. I did not know their situations or stories, but I knew that lashing out at airport employees was not helping. Those little ticketing computers cannot change regional weather events.

We live in a massive world that we can circle in mere hours. Our fellow travelers were all flying over mountains, seas, and nations, taking for granted the technology and human power that it

Epilogue: Birth and Rebirth

took to make that happen. It was a commercial flight, so I assume that most of us were not in life-or-death situations. We were surrounded by incomprehensible blessings and would end up running a little late to wherever. I saw outrage and abuse coming from people cocooned by luxury—monarchs who could not bear mild inconvenience.

And there it was! I found the character! In that moment, I saw that I was among pharaohs. I was disgusted by their behavior, yet I had more in common with them than I wanted to admit. Yes, I made generalizations and judgments about them. I apologize for that, at least where I am incorrect. Too many times have I witnessed pharaohs berating workers over minor inconveniences.

In that moment of trivial disquiet, I saw the misery of Pharaoh in the Exodus story and decided to learn from it rather than mimic it. What some might call bad luck has turned into something good. How good it is depends on how you experience and learn from this book.

Dear traveler, that is up to you. Thank you for coming.

Conversation Questions

CHAPTER 1: WHAT THINGS

1. What is your favorite kind of salad?
2. What are you made of? What do you have in common with other people? If you think of a general term like "reason," "the image of God," or "the human spirit," what specifically does that mean to you?
3. What do you have in common with nature—living things and nonliving things?
4. How do you deal with imbalance?

CHAPTER 2: THE WAYS OF WHENCE

1. Think of a time when you simply said the wrong thing. How did you misread the situation?
2. Have you had relationships that shift between the Personal, Local, and Cosmic roads—either becoming closer or more distant?
3. How do you use generalizations to navigate the world? What are some benefits and shortcomings of using those generalizations?

Conversation Questions

CHAPTER 3: THE STEPS OF HOW

1. How do you interpret the relationship between art and science?
2. How do you differentiate between knowledge, intelligence, wisdom, and understanding?

CHAPTER 4: THE CLIFFS OF WHY

1. Do you like asking the question "why?" If so, why? If not, why not?
2. Do you like answering the question "why?"

CHAPTER 5: THE SUMMIT OF WHO

1. Who are you? What relationships have helped you form that identity the most?
2. What parts of your character suit some contexts better than others?
3. Whence have you encountered the question of suffering?

CHAPTER 6: IF ONLY

1. What are some of your favorite works of fiction?
2. How have fictions formed you?

CONVERSATION QUESTIONS

CHAPTER 7: PHARAOH PHARAOH

1. Have you heard the story of Pharaoh? Whence? What do you think of and associate with him?
2. Does he remind you of anyone?

CHAPTER 8: THE MIGHTY

1. What gifts and powers have been given to you?
2. Have you ever taught yourself something? What tools and resources helped you understand the methods and goals of that something?
3. Whence have you compared yourself to someone else? How did that feel for you? Do you know how the other person felt?

CHAPTER 9: DILIGENT BLIPS

1. How do you approach the boring but necessary tasks of life? How do you cope with them? Are there techniques or tricks that have helped you?
2. Whence have your customs or manners not aligned with another person or group? How did that go?
3. What do you care about most? (Yes, you can have more than one answer.)

CHAPTER 10: CRASH AND FOAM

1. Have you seen expectations ruin reality for people? Whence has it happened to you? How were those expectations established? How were your expectations different from reality?

CONVERSATION QUESTIONS

2. Think of something in your life—like a skill set, circumstance, or relationship—that declined or disappeared. How do you feel about that? How do you wish you felt?

CHAPTER 11: LIFE IN THE WAKE

1. What experiences have you reflected upon most over the course of this book?
2. What simple wisdom have you found useful?
3. Is there any simple wisdom that you have found challenging?

www.ingramcontent.com/pod-product-compliance
Lightning Source LLC
Chambersburg PA
CBHW071218160426
43196CB00012B/2346